EMMA FOREVER

By the same author

EMMA & I

EMMA VIP

EMMA'S STORY

EMMA & CO

LIVING WITH DOGS

AFTER EMMA

EMMA
FOREVER

Sheila Hocken

LONDON
VICTOR GOLLANCZ LTD
1990

First published in Great Britain 1990
by Victor Gollancz Ltd
14 Henrietta Street, London WC2E 8QJ

© Sheila Hocken 1990

Published by arrangement with
Sphere Books Ltd

British Library Cataloguing in Publication Data
Hocken, Sheila *1946–*
Emma forever.
1. Man. Sight. Recovery. Personal adjustment of
blind persons
I. Title
362.41092

ISBN 0–575–04911–1

Typeset at The Spartan Press Ltd
Lymington, Hants
and printed in Great Britain by
St Edmundsbury Press Ltd, Bury St Edmunds, Suffolk

ILLUSTRATIONS

Following page 64

1   Showing Pip the new Dog Control notice in the park
2   Psyche shutting the door
3   Katy always walks behind me now that she can't see
4a Pip playing his favourite game, Tug
4b Pip racing to me on the "A" recall

Following page 96

5a Psyche playing dead dog
5b Dogs waiting for their walk. *Left to right*: Teak, Pip,
    Katy, Psyche and Bracken
6a It's a dog's life. *Left to right*: Katy, Mocha and
    Buttons
6b Teak waiting for Don to throw the Frisbee
7a & b Pip and I in the ring at Crufts
8   Kerensa with Psyche

INTRODUCTION

As I look out of the window I can see the lush green grass of spring, the bright yellow daffodils waving in the breeze. Most people forget to look; they simply do not appreciate sight. I never miss a moment of sight for I remember what it is like to be blind.

My mum, dad and brother Graham were all visually handicapped to some degree, so as a child I felt it was quite normal not to see very well. In fact I must have been about seven when I realised that other children did not walk into lamp-posts or put their noses right on to the page of a book to enable them to read. I suffered much teasing at school because of my need to look so closely. The other children would laugh at me and say I was like a dog smelling the pages. I learned to cope with the knocks (both mental and physical) and in many ways I think it helped me to cope with adult life.

I could have been sent away from home to a special school for the blind where I would have been equal, the same as everyone else. I would have been taught Braille and how to manage life as a blind person. In my opinion segregation does not help, whether it be for race or disability. We need to live together and accept each other's differences.

My mother had very firm ideas of how she wanted me to

be educated and that was at a local school for sighted children. It meant I missed out on the basic three Rs, for when the teacher was showing where to put commas or exclamation marks on the blackboard, or how to work out a mathematical problem, I could not see what was happening. I was allowed to go and look at the blackboard once the teacher had finished, but that was often a nuisance to the other children as I would get in their way. The blackboard stretched across the whole of one wall and I needed to walk up and down several times to follow each line of writing. Often I ended up with chalk on the end of my nose.

The one regret I have about not being able to see when I was young is that I missed so much during my teenage years. My friends were busy going to dances and dating boys. A friend took me with her to the dance hall once or twice, but going was worse than staying at home for no one asked me to dance. I am sure it was not my lack of sight which put them off but the fact that I was so terrified in the dimly lit, noisy hall that I sat in the corner with my chin tucked into my chest. I stopped going after one awful experience. My friend had met a boy there who offered her a lift home in his van. The poor girl had to tell him she was taking care of me so he extended the offer, but I had to sit in the back of the van on a dirty cold floor while they whispered sweet nothings in the front. I contented myself with going out with the dog instead of boys. I can't remember how many years of constant pleading it took for my mum to allow me to have a dog. I had made do for many years by taking other people's dogs for walks but that wasn't the same as having one of my own. I was fourteen by the time mum relented, and we acquired a seven-month-old boxer.

My favourite book as a child was *Shadow, the Sheepdog* and when bedtime came I would beg Graham to read it to me. He had more sight, and more sense, than I. Graham loved reading, although I am sure he got fed up with *Shadow, the*

8

Sheepdog. He would often say, "I'll read you some if you promise to play cricket with me tomorrow." To me that was a very difficult choice. I hated ball games of any kind because I could never see the ball coming, but I usually agreed if we could use a soft ball. Poor Graham was always lumbered with me. If I wasn't nagging him to read to me, he was taking me to school and making sure I didn't wander into the road and get run over. My mum would stand at the gate giving him instructions. "Don't let go of her hand near the road," she'd say every morning.

He never did. He held on tight until we had reached school, despite calls from his friends on the way about being a mummy's boy.

I was told by the school headmistress that I would be a telephonist. I had other ideas. I wanted to work with dogs. I have loved dogs all my life and my dream was to work in boarding kennels or anywhere with dogs. The headmistress thought that was a joke and told me I had better get used to the idea of being a telephonist as it was my only option.

She was right. I ended up sitting at a switchboard all day. Not that I hated the job: on the contrary, I enjoyed it as I was communicating with people on an equal footing for the callers had no idea I could not see.

Getting to work and back was a bit of a nightmare. I worked at the opposite side of the city from where I lived and I had to travel on two buses, changing in the busy market square. It wasn't that I did not know my way about – I knew Nottingham like the back of my hand – it was all the dangers that got in my way, like traffic and people. I accepted this frightening journey as part of my way of life. In retrospect I should have carried a white stick, if only to warn motorists I could not see them, but a white stick to me shouted of helplessness and I would never admit I needed help.

It was a home teacher for the blind who recognised my difficulties and told me I should apply for a guide-dog. Emma, a chocolate-coloured Labrador, opened the door to the world for me. She gave me independence and the confidence to go out and meet people. My first daring move was to leave home and share a flat with Anita, whom I had met at night school. Having Emma meant I could go anywhere I wanted whenever I wanted, without asking a sighted person for help. I – or should I say we? – enrolled in a writers' craft class. I had always enjoyed writing short stories and with the help of Emma I decided that learning more about being a real writer would be exciting. Anita probably would have ignored me if it had not been for Emma, for such a beautiful dog brought me admirers by the truckload and though their first approach was to Emma they would then speak to me. Anita and I became firm friends. Originally from Hull, Anita had moved to Nottingham because of her job. She lived in a dingy top-floor flat on her own and found she missed her family. After a few months of discussion we decided it would be a great idea to share a flat, all three of us.

In those days I was hardly ever at home in the flat. Life had just begun for me and I was making the most of it. I joined a few other adult education classes – pottery, make-up and beauty – and I kept up with my writers' class.

I met my husband Don because of Emma. Having a guide-dog brought me a whole new set of friends, including other blind people, and among these was George Miller, a newspaper reporter. The last job in the world you expect a blind person could do would be to report news, but George had everything worked out so he did not even have to leave his office. News was gathered by phone.

I met George in connection with guide-dogs and we would often converse over the telephone at great length about blind welfare. One evening a pal of George's joined in on the phone conversation, and the instant I heard his voice I was hooked. When Don told me he was a chiropodist I confess to having had a little giggle. I had no conception of what a chiropodist did, except that he did it with feet. To fall in love over the telephone sounds incredible, but it happened. We both felt the same way instantly and Don came to live with Emma and me. He loved Emma just as much as I did and it was definitely a case of love me love my dog.

Life for the three of us was perfect. I had almost everything anyone could wish for. I missed not being able to see, of course, but I coped with married life very well. I can't deny there were mistakes. I remember one night Don coming in for his tea and spotting an empty can on the work top.

"Good, we're having casserole stewed steak for tea. It's my favourite," he said.

"No, we aren't. It's cheese pie," I informed him.

"Well, what's this empty can doing here then?"

"It's dog food. I"ve just given it to Emma for her tea." I took the tin from him and smelled. I always had to smell food to check it was right.

"Oh dear," I said.

Don did not mind Emma eating the steak, but what worried him was what had happened to the dog food she should have had. The missing tin of Pal never turned up so I assumed we had eaten it.

Two miracles had come to me in the shape of Emma and then Don and I would have been quite happy with my life if the miracles had stopped there.

As children both Graham and I had eye operations, but they were unsuccessful. Relatives on my father's side (the eye defect was hereditary cataracts which in turn caused retina damage) had also tried and failed, so we had given up any hope of a successful eye operation. As technology moved forward so did the knowledge of the eye, and in the mid-seventies my brother was told about an eye surgeon who could probably help us. As my brother only had one eye and would be taking a risk on all or nothing, I was the one to try the operation first.

The operation was successful and at the age of twenty-nine I was looking at the world clearly for the first time. The sighted world was a kaleidoscope of brilliant colours and new discovery. I saw Don. Luckily I thought he was handsome, and I am not sure what I would have done if I had not liked the look of him. I saw sunsets and seagulls, rainbows and waves. It is now fifteen years since the operation and I still stare at everything as though I'm seeing it for the first time. If I live to be a hundred I will never take the gift of sight for granted.

I had sight, Don and Emma. Although I no longer needed Emma as a guide-dog, she was eleven years old and would have soon retired and so she became like any other pet dog. I took her for walks instead of she taking me. I also had a baby girl. Don and I both knew the risks of my eye defect being passed on to our child but we felt they were worth taking. I desperately wanted a little girl, and not only did that come true but my eye problem was not passed on to her.

Life was idyllic. I extended my love for dogs by acquiring another chocolate Labrador, Buttons, now thirteen years old, and one dog led to another. We now have seven in all. Emma died nine years ago at the ripe old age of seventeen. I still miss her. Mocha is eleven, and another chocolate Labrador. Bracken – also a chocolate Labrador – will soon be twelve, and Teak, who is eleven, is a German shorthaired pointer. We have two black Labradors, Katy, aged eight, and her daughter, Psyche, coming up for five. The youngest dog Pip, is Psyche's son, but he is a coliador. A collie jumped the garden fence and had his wicked way with Psyche while no one was looking. Pip is four years old.

I had trained my first dog back in 1960, Peggy the seven-month-old boxer, the dog I had longed for for so many years. Peggy turned out to be quite a handful as she had been rather neglected, chained up and thrown titbits to eat off the floor. I enrolled in dog training classes and that is how it started, for not only did I train Peggy but I would take other dogs for friends. The coming of Buttons and then Bracken started the dog training again and this time I could see what I was doing. I began with ordinary classes for pet owners to bring their dogs to for basic training, but I soon began to realise that training alone was not enough. Dogs that were aggressive or nervous did not seem to improve with training and I wanted to know why. For a number of years I read about animals, watched my own "pack" and attended courses on dog behaviour. Now I am able to help owners of problem dogs.

I earn my living doing the things I love most, writing and helping owners with their dog problems. Who could ask for more?

CHAPTER 1

Mocha has not changed at all from the first day she came to live with us. Her body grew, of course, but her brain never did. On arrival, at twelve weeks old, Mocha sat on the back lawn staring at the apple tree while Buttons and Bracken ran excited circles around their new playmate. She sat as if bewildered, her milk chocolate brown nose pointing skywards.

"This is little Mocha," I told Bracken and Buttons. Buttons nuzzled the pup's neck in an effort to make Mocha respond, but she sat staring, her tail swishing the lawn. I soon discovered Mocha spent most of her time daydreaming.

I became accustomed to Mocha's sedentary ways. A sweeter, better natured Labrador you could not find, but oh was she thick. I will never forget the birth of her first litter. There I was, armed with towels, hot water bottles and a huge whelping box, waiting patiently for Mocha to produce. For three days and nights I sat by the whelping box while Mocha panted and scratched up a bed into a cosy nest for her forthcoming litter and then, on August 4th at twelve o'clock, she asked to be let out into the garden. I followed her. She pottered slowly round to the dustbin, squatted down and out fell a puppy on to the cold concrete floor. Without a backward glance, Mocha walked back into the house and curled up in the whelping box. I was left to do the unwrapping of the little bundle. When I presented the pup to Mocha, she gazed at me as if to say, "Where did that come from?" Luckily she got the hang of motherhood after I had shown her what to do.

Mocha had two litters. I dared not let her have any more because her figure became an embarrassment to me. Her undercarriage never returned to normal and hung down, almost dragging on the floor. I tried taking her for long walks in the hope it would stimulate the muscles to bring her teats back up, but she didn't like the exercise and I didn't like the comments from passers-by. "Is she nursing puppies?" I would be asked and my assurances that Mocha had not had a litter of pups for years were greeted with unfriendly stares. I considered making her a pair of corsets. Especially after the other morning's episode.

All seven dogs were sleeping after their morning walk while I slaved through the monotony of housework. I envy them snoozing away the hours as I put up with the boredom of keeping the place clean. With seven dogs, we would have "dog-hair decor" if I let up on the vacuuming for a day or two. I am beginning to feel the vacuum cleaner is just an extension of my right arm. When the milkman called, I switched off the machine with relief. Buttons and Bracken stirred from their dreams and went to greet him while I looked around for the money I had left ready for him. Buttons made a spectacle of herself by throwing her big, brown body at his feet and waving her paws in the air. If she were human, she would be a brazen hussy. Bracken gave his usual woofs of greeting and pottered back to his warm place on the settee. The milkman must have smelt good that morning because Buttons tried to follow him down the drive. "If you don't come back, Buttons, you'll miss your dinner," I threatened. She lumbered past me into the lounge and I heard her jump on to the armchair, give a sigh and a low moan of contentment.

It took me about fifteen minutes to finish the carpets and then it was time to make Don's coffee.

"Nearly ready," I told him as he came through the back door.

"Where's Mocha?" His question startled me.

"What do you want Mocha for?"

"Nothing, but where is she?"

"Probably asleep in the lounge."

Don rushed into the lounge and then out to the front door. "Mocha, what are you doing out there?" he said.

Hearing Don, I abandoned the coffee making to find out what was going on. Mocha stood in the hall lashing the radiator with her tail, a dazed look on her face.

"What's the matter?" I asked Don.

"You shut Mocha outside. I have just had a patient in who asked if we had a bitch in whelp because there was one sitting outside our front door."

"I didn't shut her out. How on earth did she get there?"

"Have you opened the door at all this morning?"

"Only to pay the milkman." It dawned on me then that she must have slipped out while I was looking for the money. I wasn't worried about Mocha getting out on to the main road, even though we have no gate at the front. None of our dogs would dream of leaving home. What did worry me was what people would think when seeing a poor dog looking as if she were nursing a litter sitting outside the front door waiting to be let in by some dreadfully cruel owner.

"I tried to explain to the patient that Mocha did not have pups and she must have got out there by accident. I knew you wouldn't have let her out there but I don't think he believed me, and when I went on to explain about Mocha's mental capacity and reluctance to exercise I am sure he thought I was spinning him a shaggy dog story."

"Really, Mocha," I chastised, "my name will be mud around the neighbourhood."

I stood in front of her wagging a finger. She didn't even give me a glance as she walked round me and leapt onto the armchair that Buttons was already occupying. Buttons gave a grunt as Mocha's bulk landed on her. She tried a growling protest but Mocha was oblivious as she sat with half-closed eyes on top of Buttons. Eventually Buttons gave in and squirmed from underneath. Mocha simply flopped down and began to snore.

If Mocha has not been senile all her life, I am sure it is happening now. Her response has always been slow but nowadays she seems to forget what she is doing, even when eating her dinner. That very afternoon she sat gazing at the freezer, ignoring her half-eaten dinner.

"Hurry up, Mocha, all the others finished ages ago."

I heard her tail swish across the floor but she still stared fixedly at the freezer. I tapped her bowl, but she ignored me, stood up and ambled to the back door.

If any of the other dogs left their food half eaten I would be at the vet's with the speed of light, but Mocha is different. She sometimes gives up on her dinner for no apparent reason. The next day, Sunday, Mocha appeared a little lethargic – but when was Mocha energetic? So I still didn't feel concerned about her condition, but on Monday morning I became alarmed. Mocha lay on the chair panting, and when I offered her a piece of chicken she took it into her mouth and then dropped it as if it was all too much of an effort. I rang the vet and made an immediate appointment. By the time Betty arrived to take me Mocha had deteriorated beyond belief. We had to carry her into the car and when we reached the surgery she had become a dead weight and I had to call for the vet to help me to carry her in.

She lay on the table, oblivious to her surroundings, as the vet examined her.

"You have one very sick dog here," the vet told me. "Her temperature is below normal and she is very jaundiced."

After answering a few questions about the last couple of days, the vet could not give a prognosis. "We will need to do some tests. I just hope we can save her."

I was stunned. It had been so quick. What I had thought was Mocha's normally "can't-be-bothered" attitude over her food was the onset of this terrible illness. I went home without her.

Seven dogs is quite a lot of canines and one would think one dog either way would not make much difference, especially Mocha. No one really notices her. She is just around, daydreaming. She never begs to go out for a walk. In fact, by the time she gets to the park all she wants to do is sit down and let the world pass her by. Despite the other six dogs the house seemed empty, void of Mocha. I was convinced she was going to die and so was the vet. I tried to continue as normal at home, but it is difficult to work through tears. I was devastated. I couldn't believe Mocha could go down so quickly with this mysterious illness. I rang the vet, in fear and trepidation, later that day to hear she was still alive but tests had been taken and rushed to the lab. All we could do was sit back and wait.

If I am to be honest with myself, I have never felt particularly attached to Mocha. Oh yes, I am fond of her, but she has always simply been there. Now I realised how much her being there meant to me. My hands shook so much the next morning that I could hardly dial the vet's number. What if she had died in the night?

"How is Mocha?" I managed to croak.

"Still about the same."

"Have any of the results come back?"

"No, I was just going to ring the lab."

I could tell the vet was trying not to give anything away. I knew he was convinced that Mocha had not got long.

Tuesday passed in a haze of fear. Every time the telephone rang, my heart leapt into my mouth in case it was the call I was dreading. On Wednesday morning the vet told me I could collect Mocha and he would give me the results of the tests.

Doctors and vets have an awful habit of spreading foreboding by their reluctance to discuss anything over the telephone. By the time I arrived at the surgery I was convinced they were letting me take Mocha home to die. The vet ushered me into his surgery and began to pore over some papers.

"Are those the lab results?" I asked tentatively.

"Yes, but they still don't have the answer. There has been a mass destruction of red corpuscles."

That told me nothing. "Does that give any clues?"

"It could be a number of things."

"Such as?"

"It can be symptomatic of leukaemia, or cancer of some sort, or liver trouble."

"What do you think?" It is so hard to pin medical people down and I wanted to know what I was up against.

"It could be a growth on the liver."

"And if it is, can you do anything?"

He shook his head. "Mocha does seem a bit better this morning. She has eaten a little. The only thing I can say is get her home, look after her and take the next few days as they come."

To me, that meant Mocha didn't have long and there was nothing I or anyone else could do about it. Mocha greeted me gently and plodded slowly after me to the car. On reaching home, she hauled herself into her favourite chair, gave a big sigh of contentment and closed her eyes. I dared not leave her alone. I hardly dared blink my eyes in case something happened to her. As the day progressed, so did Mocha: from eating mouthfuls of chicken to having a potter round the garden. I stayed up late with her that night. She seemed to be feeling quite well – maybe a remission. When she began to snore blissfully, I decided to go to bed. I hadn't slept much for two nights and I was exhausted.

When the radio alarm switches itself on in the mornings, this is the signal for Katy to get out of her own bed and jump on to ours. She has a little roll and a snort and then lies between Don and I, fixing her gaze on Don, willing him to get up and take her and the others out for their walk around the woods. On Thursday morning, I was awoken, gasping for breath. I felt as if I was drowning in tepid water that kept washing over me like waves. When I opened my eyes there were two big brown eyes staring straight at me. A large brown nose met mine and the tepid wave came again. It was Mocha's tongue. She obviously felt much better.

She progressed steadily over the next few days and our visit to the vet on the following Monday was greeted by, "Which dog is this?" He didn't even recognise her.

"It's Mocha. What do you think?"

"I think you're having me on," he said, and smiled. "Is it really Mocha?" After convincing himself I was telling the truth, he said, "You know, we had three dogs in over the weekend with exactly the same symptoms and they all died."

Mocha jumped up and down on the spot, as if to alert us to the fact that she was alive and kicking.

I find it very difficult to believe that disasters have a purpose in life, but I try to look for the silver lining. Mocha's illness had a silver lining; not for me, but for a little mongrel called Mindi, who would be dead if it had not been for Mocha's traumatic experience.

I wrote a piece about Mocha's mysterious illness in my pets' column for the Nottingham *Evening Post*, hoping other dog owners might be able to throw some light on the subject. Perhaps other dogs had suffered and recovered, or the local vets could have discovered more about the illness. I find it useful to ask readers to share their experiences as this enables me to gather information. But instead of receiving letters, I had a call from an owner in terrible distress. Sue Evans was battling to save her dog's life. Mindi, a shaggy little mongrel, had been ill for about three weeks. Sue's vet had tried various treatments to no avail, and, on Mindi's last visit to the vet, it was suggested that Mindi had leukaemia and should be put down to save further suffering. I was Mindi's last hope.

"I was going to take Mindi to have her put down when my husband read your column."

Sue was registered blind and unable to see to read. Although Mindi was not a guide-dog, she gave Sue comfort in the house and the thought of losing her little dog was unbearable.

"My vet says it's cruel to keep her alive, but she has exactly the same symptoms as Mocha. I don't want to lose her. Can you help me?"

Poor Sue was distressed. I didn't want to give her false hope, especially as my vet had told me about the other dogs with the same symptoms which had died. And what if Mindi was suffering? I would advise Sue to put her down if she did have leukaemia. The disease is common in cats but quite rare in dogs.

"What can I do?" Sue said.

"Maybe you should get a second opinion."

"Am I allowed to do that? I mean, will another vet take Mindi on? I thought they were like doctors."

"If you are paying the bill you can choose who you like. And what is most important to you, offending a vet or Mindi's life?"

With that thought in mind, Sue took Mindi to another vet. Although unable to diagnose the illness, the new vet pulled the little dog through to perfect health. I wish Mocha could understand that her illness saved Mindi's life. I get a warm glow when I think about that little dog.

CHAPTER 2

I was just beginning to drift off to sleep, covered with the warm pink feeling that comes just before slumber, when I felt Don's comforting arm envelop me.

"Poor Katy, I wish you wouldn't look at me like that."

I was suddenly wide awake. "Like what?" I asked.

"Sorry petal, I thought you were asleep. It's Katy. When I tell her to get off the bed and go to her beanbag, she throws her ears forward and furrows up her brow. She makes her face look as if all the skin is going to gather at the end of her nose and then fall off. It makes me feel guilty."

"Why should you feel guilty? It's your part of the bed she gets ensconced in."

"Yes, I know, but I get this awful feeling that Katy wishes I wouldn't come to bed."

"Dogs don't think like that and, anyway, even if they did you are the boss."

"It's not a resentful look she gives me. That I could cope with. No, it's piteous. I find it hard."

Katy sleeps in our bedroom. I could not bear the thought of a bedroom that didn't vibrate gently through the night with the sound of snoring Labrador. It had become a ritual that if I went to bed first then Katy could sleep on the bed until Don came up, and then she was relegated to her beanbag. Don began to suffer guilt complexes about moving her, so I brought the biscuit routine in. Every night, along with the cups of milk and teabags for our Teasmaid, there would be a biscuit which I strategically placed in Katy's view on the shelf. The biscuit was given to her, on her beanbag, when Don came to bed. This cured any form of remorse Don had about moving Katy as, being a Labrador, food comes before anything. Now as soon as she hears Don climbing the stairs she is alert, nose twitching, staring at the biscuit, ready to make the jump from our bed to hers.

It is quite amazing what we humans do to make us feel better in a dog–person relationship. Don felt guilty and mean for pushing Katy off the bed when, in truth, this type of action is a good example of keeping the correct balance. Katy has no aggression or desire to lead a pack, whether it be dogs or humans, and that is one of the reasons why she is allowed upstairs in preference to the other dogs. A dominant dog would soon try to take advantage of being treated as a higher ranking member. In fact, a dominant dog would more than likely become aggressive if forced to move off a bed. But not little Katy. Not only did she enjoy the biscuit offered her, but she loved the new bed I had bought for her – a large beanbag.

Every night there would be a battle with the beanbag, as she fought to get it under control. To watch this ritual war dance take place you would be forgiven for believing the beanbag to be a living entity. Katy can make the whole thing spring into life. She buries her nose in the middle and pulls upwards with her teeth while her front paws are gathering and digging. The bed changes into different shapes as Katy dances with it around the bedroom floor. Although Katy loves her bed, I feel it only fair to warn anyone who is thinking of buying one for their dog that they are un-believably noisy, especially in the dead of night. It sounds like ten tons of gravel being off-loaded into your ear.

I put up with this inconvenience because I was so happy to see (and hear) Katy so mobile. At the age of five she had begun to limp on her right front leg. After X-rays, it was diagnosed as arthritis. Drugs seemed to be the only option, but the thought of keeping Katy on drugs for the rest of her life was very distressing and I looked about for alternatives. I tried all the homeopathic remedies, but to no avail. One morning I received a letter that was going to give me the answer to Katy's problem. I get many letters through writing a pets' column mostly asking for help or advice, but this one was different. A success story about a little Sheltie dog who had been involved in a road accident, causing severe damage to his front leg. His owner was advised to have the leg amputated, but she was appalled at this and sought other help. Like me, she had investigated various types of treatment, none successful until she heard of a physiotherapist who practised acupuncture for pets. After a few treatments the Sheltie was beginning to use the injured leg. I traced the physiotherapist immediately to ask if she could offer help with Katy.

Janet Sewell, a qualified physiotherapist for humans, had begun treating dogs when one of her own pets sustained a spine injury and her vet had been unable to offer treatment. Firstly Janet had just used physiotherapy with her dog, and then acupuncture.

As with any new or alternative treatment I was sceptical, but I decided I had to give it a try, not only for Katy's sake but also for Katy's son, Logan, owned by a friend, Rosemary. Logan had suffered with his shoulder from early puppyhood. A shoulder defect had set up arthritis (one of the reasons I gave up breeding was the arthritis problem in Labradors). We both made the appointment to take the dogs for their first treatment. I know I felt very nervous about the whole thing. What would Katy do when a stranger started to stick needles in her and, more to the point, what would I do?

I confess to being rather squeamish when it comes to my own pets. I have actually watched operations on dogs at my vet's and found it fascinating, but I didn't know or love the dog that was being cut open.

Rosemary and I arrived at the house for the dogs' treatment with some trepidation. We were all made welcome in Janet's comfortable sitting room where the dogs stretched out in front of the fire. Janet's sitting room was like a home from home, with show trophies her Golden Retrievers had won and paintings of dogs hung over the stone fireplace.

Janet sat on the floor with the dogs, gently examining their arthritic joints. When I saw the first needle being inserted into Katy's shoulder my stomach turned over and I screwed my eyes up, waiting for Katy's reaction. It was silence. She just lay there, completely unperturbed. Logan, too, accepted the treatment without complaint. I feel sure the dogs were so calm because of the relaxed atmosphere. Janet's sitting room bore no resemblance to a vet's surgery.

The next day Katy was showing a marked improvement in her mobility. During the previous few months she had had difficulty climbing the stairs and had stopped jumping up on to the bed. Now she was taking the stairs at a gallop and leaping on to the bed. Logan took a while longer to show an improvement but, after about six treatments, both dogs were using their arthritic shoulders freely.

The alternative treatments in humans are often marred by a placebo effect. One can't say that with animals and I will, in the future, keep an open mind as regards alternative treatments available both to dogs and people.

CHAPTER 3

At the age of forty I felt I had achieved nothing in life, academically speaking. When I heard teenagers answering questions on game shows, such as "How far is it to the moon?" or "Where is the deepest ocean trench?", it made me realise I was totally ignorant of such matters. Added to this fact, I wanted to improve my knowledge of human and canine behaviour, so I decided to take an Open University degree.

My aim was psychology, but I was informed that everyone wishing to take a degree with the OU has to take a foundation course first. As none of the courses seemed applicable to psychology, I decided to take science because that was my best subject at school. I didn't imagine it would be easy, but I also didn't realise just how lacking in knowledge I was.

Don thought I was crackers. He pointed out I wouldn't have time to study. I couldn't argue with that. I am constantly complaining I have too much to do, but I was beginning to feel old and I really wanted to prove to myself that I had the ability to achieve something in the academic world. Don put it down to mid-life crisis but, nevertheless, he offered to help where he could. Working from home seems easy when you go out to work every day, but in practice it takes great feats of will to work or study. It would be easy if I could lock myself away from the intrusions of everyday life. Yesterday, for example, it took me two hours to make the bed because of the regular round of doorbell callers, milkmen and the like, and the phone. I would love to ignore these intrusions and lock myself in the garden shed, but I can't. One of the phone calls was from a lady who could hardly talk for sobbing.

"My dog has just attacked me. What can I do? My husband says he should be put down, but we all love him too much. What am I going to do?"

That call took half an hour to deal with. None of my phone calls ever seems straightforward.

The tutors at the OU were very helpful when I explained my visual difficulties to them. Roz was elected as my personal tutor and she visited me to explain how everything works.

"You will need a basic knowledge of maths."

"Yes, well that's what I've got. A very basic knowledge."

"It's okay," she assured me. "You will receive some maths books covering the material you need for the course."

Roz had misled me. I know she didn't mean to but her understanding of "a basic knowledge" and mine were streets apart.

"What about visual work? Do you think I can cope?"

"I'm sure you can and there will be study group meetings in Nottingham to help you."

I know what my problem is and I have always been guilty of it. I exude confidence, ignore my own faults and lack of knowledge. I am easily led into thinking I am more intelligent than I really am and I seem to convince other people, too. When the maths books arrived I grabbed them with enthusiasm, intent on studying them before the course started. After all, maths was just logic, so it would be simple once I got the hang of it.

I skimmed through the contents – algebra, radians, scientific notation – it was completely foreign to me. The instructions for using a calculator must be simple, I reckoned, so I dug out my pocket calculator and opened my maths book. The instructions seemed clear enough. "Put the first set of figures into your calculator then press pi." I couldn't find a button on my calculator that said "pi". I tried another set. "Now press square root." I couldn't find one of those on my machine either. Poor Roz, she must have thought me a right bird-brain when I told her my calculator didn't have the buttons the maths book said it should have.

"You need a scientific one," she informed me, with a deep sigh.

When that arrived I was horrified. It had a thick book of instructions which I had to fathom out before I learnt how to switch on. Even with a calculator at my disposal, the maths exercises were, to me, like trying to swim through treacle.

I never imagined that my decision to take this course would affect our lives so much. I thought I could quietly work away on my studies and no one would be any the wiser, but it doesn't work like that at all. The other day, when Don came in for his tea, he found me staring at a set of keys hanging from a hook in the ceiling by a green piece of string. My daughter, Kerensa, sat on the kitchen stool, watch in hand. I hardly noticed Don enter as I followed the swing of the keys, counting the seconds out loud.

"Any tea on the go, petal?"

"Fifteen, wait a minute, sixteen . . . "

For a moment, Don stood taking in the scene. I am sure he thought I had finally flipped. Calmly, and without a trace of panic in his tone, he asked me what I was doing.

"I'm timing these keys. I'm not cooking them. I need to know how long it takes for the keys to swing ten times."

"Of course you do, petal. What's for tea?"

"Now." I told Kerensa. "That's twenty-one seconds."

Don leaned across me to fill the kettle and I think I heard him muttering something about starting "a home for the bewildered".

"Right. Now we can have tea," I said. Explaining to Don that the keys were an experiment for the OU course, I pushed the bread into the toaster.

"Thank goodness for that," he said. "I've heard of women going totally potty at your time of life and I couldn't face the thought of visiting you every weekend at Saxondale." (That's the local psychiatric hospital.)

In the evening I studied while Don watched the snooker. The first lesson was about our star system. I looked carefully at the drawings depicting the earth orbiting the sun and the moon orbiting the earth. It suddenly struck me how precarious our situation here on earth is.

"Look, petal," I began, interrupting Don's concentration on the snooker match. He averted his eyes from the screen for a split second.

"Um, yes . . . very interesting."

"Petal, do look. It's very important."

Poor Don. I wouldn't leave him alone to enjoy the snooker. He managed to drag his gaze away from the screen to focus on the book I was pushing under his nose.

"Here, this is us, the earth. This is the moon, which is orbiting. And there is the sun and we travel round it once a year."

"Good, it hasn't changed recently," he said and grinned.

"No, but it could. I mean there's nothing out there holding us up. What happens if we drop out of orbit, or the moon suddenly decides to shoot off somewhere?"

"Don't worry about it. It has been all right for millions of years . . . Oh dear, poor old Denis has been knocked out."

I do like Denis Taylor, but at that moment I was more worried about life on earth. "Yes, I know, but that is what's worrying me. It can't go on forever. One day it's just going to fall apart."

Don was far too interested in the TV, so I decided to worry about the fate of the universe on my own for a while. I blundered on through the lesson until I reached the paragraph that told me I should now fully understand the orbiting circles of the planets and moon and why we only saw one side of the moon all the time. I didn't. I leafed back through the lesson to reread the relevant details. "Due to the orbit and axis of spin, only one part of the moon would be visible no matter where one was on earth." In desperation, I turned to Don,

"Do you know why we only see one side of the moon? It says here that it's due to the axis of spin and the tilt of orbit. It doesn't make sense to me."

"Angles, that's what causes it. Very deceptive are angles."

"Yes, but I still don't understand it."

"Can't you just accept the fact, petal?" he asked, his attention still riveted to the green snooker table on the screen.

"Taking an Open University degree does not mean I just have to accept the fact, I must be able to understand it."

Don gave up any idea of watching television and turned towards me. "I'll show you." He picked up his packet of cigars in one hand and tankard of beer in the other. "Pretend this is the moon" – he waved his packet of cigars in the air – "and this is the earth." He lifted his tankard.

"I'll try, but do forgive me if I laugh at the thought of the earth being orbited by a packet of cigars."

"Now, watch carefully. The moon is tilted like this." He moved the cigars in the air. "And the earth is tilted like this." He turned his beer tankard on its side. The brown liquid began to stream out over Mocha's head. Any normal dog would have jumped up in surprise, having half a pint of best bitter poured into a left ear, but not Mocha. She gave an extra large snore and turned over. It took her about five minutes to gain full awareness that she felt uncomfortable. She sat up and began to stare at the ceiling and then her warm brown eyes rested on me with a puzzled expression.

"It wasn't my fault, Mocha. The earth leaked."

CHAPTER 4

My mum was singing along to *Sing Something Simple* on the radio, waving her arms in time to the music. "Underneath the arches on cobblestones I lay . . . " she warbled and when the singers changed to "Maresy dotes and dosey dotes and little lamsey divey" she sang out even louder.

Normally I hated *Sing Something Simple* but, watching my mum enjoying herself so much, I began to sing along too. At that moment it seemed like a taste of heaven but then I woke up to reality, tears streaming down my face. It had been a dream, a very cruel dream. Mum couldn't sing along to anything any more because she had become profoundly deaf.

As long as I can remember my mum had been quite deaf; but with the help of a hearing aid she had managed and, true to her temperament, I had never once heard her complain of her misfortune. Quite the opposite, in fact: she was always willing to see the funny side of things. Sentences would get so ravelled up by the time mum received them that she often had us in stitches at what she thought we had said.

"Where has dad gone to tonight?" I asked.

"Never!" Mum looked astonished.

"Never what?"

"Don couldn't have got involved in anything like that, could he?"

"Wait a minute, mum. What did you think I said?"

"That Don was involved in a gunfight."

She could see from the way I was rolling around laughing that she had misheard and began laughing with me.

Or, "What would you like me to fetch you from the shops?"

"No, I don't want any foreign meat."

Mum thought I had said, "Would you like some French pork chops?"

Now not only had her hearing gone, but her sight had deteriorated to such a degree that she could no longer read or watch television. I lay there in the dark silence of the night, which seemed to reinforce the world my mum was living in. She was trapped in a dark silence which was getting more and more difficult to penetrate, so much so that we were now having to write words on her hand.

My mum's eye problem was caused by scarred corneas from measles when she was a child. Cornea grafts were unheard of in those days and, in the fifties, when such operations had become a possibility, mum was "not bothered". She had enough sight to cope with life and she didn't hanker for anything better for herself. But things were becoming drastic. We could not let her suffer in a prison of silent darkness.

The virtues I had always admired about her were now becoming annoying obstacles. I can never remember her buying something for herself because she wanted it. If she bought clothes or shoes it was because she needed them. I will never forget how we struggled in the fifties and yet, as a child, I had no conception of the real difficulties that faced my parents. We had a little drapery shop on St Ann's Well Road, notably the roughest area in Nottinghamshire. Dad's sight was poor and limited his ability to work. I think he received survival pay from his job at the Blind Institution. Mum looked after the shop. In retrospect I can understand what a terrible trial that must have been, for her poor sight and hearing kept her on edge whenever a customer came in.

No one had much money to throw about, especially not the residents of the St Ann's area. The shop didn't make much and at night mum would supplement our income by knitting jumpers on her knitting machine. I often joke about life in those days, but times were tough. I remember being called into the headmistress's study and questioned about my shoes. They were literally dropping off my feet. It was not the done thing to admit poverty so I told the headmistress I had made a mistake that morning and put on the wrong pair. When I told her what had happened, mum was upset but somewhat relieved when I related my explanation to the headmistress. Mum had not known about the state of my shoes. It hadn't bothered me they were falling apart. I don't know where the money came from but the next day I had a new pair of shoes.

Amid this struggle against poverty, my mum still managed to be charitable to an old lady called Mrs Jarrot. Mrs Jarrot was "the cat lady". Her little terraced house was filled to the brim with cats other people had turfed out, probably because they couldn't afford to feed them; Mrs Jarrot, a pensioner, with no relatives and crippled by arthritis, certainly could not afford it either. Every week, my mum would send me up to Mrs Jarrot with a heavy bag full of groceries and I was instructed to take no money, however much it was pressed upon me.

I was about nine years old at the time. I didn't want to lug heavy bags up the road to an old woman who had a house full of cats. I would much rather be playing with my friends. But mum had done a good job of instilling moral standards into me and now I am glad I went once a week, without complaint. I would sit in the tiny living room of that dark, terraced house. Cats would climb all over me. The smell was overpowering. I always itched and scratched on the way home.

There was usually a new litter of kittens to see and when they had been fussed and petted I would go out into the back yard, for Mrs Jarrot had something we didn't have – soil and flowers. Flowers fascinated me. No one near us had a garden and flowers were a luxury. To buy food and clothes was far more important. Nowadays, when Don buys me flowers, which is nearly every Friday, it makes me feel secure. While I nursed a few kittens, Mrs Jarrot would make the tea. It took her about five minutes to get from the back yard to the tiny scullery, so crippled was she with arthritis. My mum sent food for the cats and for Mrs Jarrot. She knew the old lady would feed the cats in preference to herself, so she worked on the assumption that if the cats were well provided for Mrs Jarrot would eat what was left. Kit-e-Kat, cornflakes, milk and margarine (no one ate butter, not where we lived) were survival rations until I could visit her again.

I am sure my mum's caring nature stems from her own past hardships. Being orphaned at about ten years of age, she spent much of her childhood in children's homes. From the stories she still relates to me, the children's homes of the thirties were evil places. If I thought the matrons from those homes were still alive, I would personally seek them out and claim revenge for my mum.

The children were up at six a.m., working before school, scrubbing floors, leading the old black fireplaces, sewing and cooking. Those homes always managed to convey normality and goodness to visitors. A large jar of sweets was kept on a shelf, in full view of visitors. The children there were only allowed to look at the jar, they were never given a sweet. They were regarded as slaves who made life easy for the women who ran the homes.

When mum became old enough to leave the home, she still had nowhere to go. Her teenage years were spent in institutions or with friends until she married. A life of crime is often attributed to an early unsettled life and yet my mum is completely honest and has always had so much love to give. At least she made sure her children's lives would be happy.

The more dad, my brother Graham and I insisted that mum should see an eye specialist, the more she seemed to turn inwards, as if she had no right to seek sight, as if she had to put up with whatever the fates threw at her. Nineteen-eighty-eight seemed an endless year of crying for my mum. I often think that tears and distress must run out eventually, but they don't always.

Christmas 1987 was overshadowed by the fact that mum did not take part in our annual shopping expedition to Nottingham. Every year, Kerensa and I met her in the city to shop and have lunch. Often Graham would join us for the lunch. I am one of those people who hate change and any upset in my regular pattern leaves me very depressed. Graham met us in town that year and, although it was nice to have lunch with him, mum's absence was a painful reminder of what she must be suffering. I didn't blame her for not coming. What pleasure could there be in shopping when you couldn't see or hear?

Over the past few years her hearing had diminished temporarily but then returned again for no apparent reason. When I rang her it was often difficult to make her understand what I was saying. Don always knew when I was having trouble getting through as he would hear the familiar shout, "Can you hear me, mother?" When she heard that, we had a little laugh about it – it became our call sign. Increasingly, it became more and more difficult to communicate. It could be the fault of the hearing aid and, despite the fact she had already investigated this possibility, I offered to go with her to the Hearing-Aid Centre at the beginning of December.

I find that communication is far more difficult when someone cannot hear, not only because it takes an effort to repeat words constantly but the general public have no thought or consideration for the deaf. Being blind is so easily understood. One only needs to shut one's eyes to comprehend the difficulties involved, but deafness can often make a person look stupid. I felt confident I could get mum fixed up with a better hearing aid if I went with her and explained the situation. She probably needed a more powerful aid.

"This hearing aid is no good at all," I told the young woman at the centre. "Surely you have something more powerful?" Mum sat patiently waiting; she has the patience of a saint. If I were her, I know I would be ranting and raving at my predicament and demanding someone do something to restore my hearing.

"There isn't a hearing aid that will help your mother now."

"What do you mean 'now'?" I asked, rather sharply. It helped me cope with the situation to be annoyed with her.

"The hearing has gone, the nerves have worn out . . . there is nothing we can do to help."

For a minute or two, I found the statement impossible to take in. She was telling me that my mum would never hear again, that for the rest of her life she couldn't listen to the television or talk to me on the telephone, hear someone knocking at the door, go shopping on her own . . . or just simply listen. Much worse than those thoughts going through my mind was how to tell mum. I had to write it down for her. She could just make out big letters in felt-tip pen.

There is something really awesome, final, about writing such a statement. I sat wondering how to go about it. I wanted to pass the buck, as they say, and tell this young woman facing me to write down those terrible words. "Nothing can be done. You will be deaf forever." But I couldn't ask her. The lump in my throat was too big. I was biting my lip hard to stop myself crying. There was no option. I wrote, "AT THE MOMENT THEY CAN'T HELP, BUT MAYBE AFTER CHRISTMAS WE COULD TRY AGAIN." I had to leave a margin of hope. I didn't want to be the one who gave mum a life sentence of deafness, and that is the way it felt at the time.

We redoubled our efforts to encourage mum to do something about an eye operation. In the end, we were rather underhand about it. Finding we could not persuade her by telling her what she was missing and what she could have, we changed our tack and told her it wasn't fair on us that we could not communicate, and appealed to her sense of family commitment. That worked, and eventually she agreed to see an eye surgeon. Dad, Graham and I decided to go as well since the outcome was important to us all. The surgeon was astonished to see someone without hearing or sight and found it hard to believe mum had simply accepted the situation. So concerned was he that, there and then, he contacted the East Grinstead Hospital where the cornea bank is and where some of the top cornea graft surgeons in the world work. Not only would mum need a cornea graft but also a cataract removal. The surgeon explained to us that she stood a much better chance of success at East Grinstead. The appointment was made for her to have the operation.

Going into hospital at any time is not very nice, but almost unthinkable when you are unable to communicate and take in what is happening around you. Luckily, the staff at the hospital realised the difficulties and it was arranged that dad would stay with her. It was September 1988, a good month to have an eye operation, as it was September when I got my sight. I felt this to be a very good omen and, as a family, we were due for some good omens.

There are times when I think that I – or rather the rest of my family – are suffering for the sins of the fathers, or maybe my good fortune in life. One always feels good luck has to be paid for. Nineteen-eighty-eight had not been very nice for Graham. He had spent some time in hospital with a growth in the bowel, but by September he had a clean bill of health and I turned my powers of worrying to mum's operation. I knew it would be successful and when Dad rang to say she could see bright colours across the ward I danced about the house and garden, singing with sheer relief and joy.

What a wonderful Christmas we had that year! Mum, Kerensa and I had a wonderful day's shopping. Graham met us for lunch and took us to a nice little restaurant he had found. I was in seventh heaven sitting there, tucking into a huge plate of scampi and chips and telling Graham, between mouthfuls, how we had spent the morning, mum looking in the shops and asking me if I could see notices miles away. Admittedly, her not being able to hear me was still sad, but at least she could read my notes.

I am so thankful I didn't know then what the future held and that would be the last time we would meet for our special lunch.

CHAPTER 5

My burning ambition has always been to qualify one of my
dogs for the obedience competition at Crufts Dog Show.
Every year only a very select handful of dogs qualify for the
obedience competition. In the breed section there are
around twelve thousand dogs, as the qualification for breed
is only one first place at a championship show. The
obedience has to be worked towards with many first places.
Apart from the cream of competition dogs, there is now a
team event. Two dogs from each class are selected to
represent the area in the four main levels of obedience and
Pip was in the running for the Midlands team. He had won a
novice and had numerous seconds during the season, which
put him in a good position. Encouraged by my friends, I
decided to put his name forward, half hoping we would not
get chosen. It may have been my ambition to get to the big
ring at Crufts, but now it was becoming a possibility could I
cope with the nerve-racking experience I knew it would be?
Once my application had been accepted on paper we had to
have an audition, or run-through, in front of three judges to
assess our capabilities to work in the team.

I was incredibly nervous as I put Pip through his paces,
knowing that my slightest mistake would be picked up.

"Very nice," Roy, the team organiser, commented, on the

completion of the test. "We'll contact you by letter in a week or two."

I smiled graciously and left the ring.

"Well?" Rosemary asked me. "What did they say?"

"They'll write to me," I told her. "I'm sure that means we haven't made the grade."

Rosemary looked very disappointed. She shares as much in my show successes as I do in hers, especially as she has Katy's son Logan.

"Never mind. Maybe my nerves wouldn't have stood up to it."

Over the next few weeks I completely forgot about Crufts as I was convinced I had received the brush-off. And then, one morning, I opened a letter headed "Midlands Obedience Team":

"Dear Sheila,

I am very pleased to inform you that you and Pip have been chosen to represent the Midlands team at Crufts . . . "

I could hardly believe it. We had actually been chosen. Pip, a cross-bred accident, had made the big time. The next eight weeks were spent in serious training for the big day in February. Pip was in his element. The more training we did, the more he could play with his ball. The more I learn about dogs and their reaction to motivation, the more interesting and involved the training becomes. To the ordinary dog owner, training a dog means teaching it to sit and walk on a lead, and many owners are not even capable of doing that simple thing. But then why should they be? Dog training is an art and everyone cannot be expected to spend hours motivating their dog to work for them.

I spend hours not only working with the dogs, but thinking how best to approach a certain problem or new exercise. The key to success is getting the dog to want to carry out an order correctly. Far too many people, pet owners and trainers alike, lose sight of the fact that dogs do not understand English. Owners frequently get annoyed with their dogs because they do not follow a simple order, such as "Down" or "Stay". Men are the worst culprits when it comes to giving a little understanding. The problem with most men dog owners is their motives for having a dog. Too many male chauvinists have a dog so they can boss it around. I am sure this stems, in part, from the structure of society now. Women were always the brunt of the chauvinist male, but now women know better and stand up for their rights. The male bully needs to feel he can be boss, so he gets a dog and tries to prove his manhood by dominating the poor animal. I get dozens of men coming to the training classes who dislike the idea of "bribing" their dog to obey a command. "Why should I give him a titbit for lying down?" they want to know. "The dog should do as I say, never mind the bribery." I treat this attitude with the contempt it deserves and ask if they go out to work and, if so, do they get a regular wage for working? The usual reply to this is, "Of course I get paid. I'm not working for nothing."

"Exactly!" I shout triumphantly. "So why should your dog work for nothing?" That normally shuts them up.

I know that teaching a dog to understand and comply takes time and patience and each command must be fully understood. No one can read unless they first learn the alphabet and, with a dog, he can't be expected to obey unless he fully understands the word. How many times have I heard an owner complain, "My dog only does as he is told when he feels like it"? To prove to my training class the other day that their dogs often did not understand commands, I tried an experiment. Every owner was told to point to the ground and tell their dog to "Rhubarb". Every single dog lay down. That proved to me that the dogs were following signals and not commands. Next I asked the owners to stand up straight and not move a muscle and give the "Down" command to their dogs. All the dogs sat looking up at their owners with puzzled looks. Not one dog understood the actual word "Down".

I know that Pip will do his best to obey a command because, if he gets it right, he is allowed to play with his ball. If he gets the command wrong then it is my fault and I need to rethink my methods. I did a lot of thinking about Crufts. I so wanted to be a credit to the team. One thing worried me for a while, and that was the benches at Crufts. Each dog has to be tied up on a bench and most owners use benching chains for this purpose. The chains tend to bang on the sides of the bench and make a loud noise, one which Pip did not like the sound of. For some time I considered the problem and then I hit on the answer – make Pip like the sound of chains rattling.

Every day for the two weeks before Crufts, Pip was called to eat his dinner by the sound of a chain rattling on his dish. Now, if he hears that same sound, he comes running, thinking dinner is served. Working in the big ring at Crufts could be a frightening experience for a dog, with crowds of people shouting and cheering. At a normal dog show there are no crowds, only fellow competitors. I covered that by getting friends at the training club to make as much noise as possible while Pip and I went through our paces. If Pip showed any fear when cheers and applause burst out I threw his ball. By the time Crufts loomed, he would leap up and down in excitement if he heard people making a lot of noise, expecting his ball.

Not only did I need to work with Pip on my own, but I had to attend pre-Crufts training sessions. Everyone chosen for the Midlands team met at Stoneleigh on three consecutive Saturday mornings in January. Stoneleigh was an ideal venue, as the sheds used for cattle and horses were about the nearest we could get to simulate the acoustics and atmosphere at Earl's Court. The cream of the Midlands trainers came to help us polish up our presentation. It was a lovely cheerful get-together as we were not competing against each other but, as one team, we would be pulling together for the Midlands.

Stoneleigh is not an ideal venue for me, however, because it is rather dark and I have problems seeing in restricted lighting, but I was hardly going to mention this to Roy Page, the team organiser. I wasn't going to blow my chances of getting to Crufts. Luckily for me, my allotted trainer knew about my visual problems. Denis Bradley, the trainer, and his wife, Margaret, had become firm friends over the years I had competed. The first time I met Margaret was when she judged me and Katy. After I had completed the round she complimented me, saying how nicely Katy worked. "But oh dear," she had added, "you can't walk straight, can you? Try to look where you are going when you work in the ring." The best way to get over any disability is to laugh about it and I did just that, telling Margaret I had trouble seeing where I was going anyway, let alone in a strange place.

The rings for obedience are roped off in a large square so the competitor can follow the left, right and forward commands within the square. My problem is I can't see the ropes, not until I walk into them. Margaret became a godsend to me at dog shows as she had a knack of knowing when I would have problems in the ring. "When you do the about-turn line yourself up with that tree and you will be walking straight," she'd say. Her bits of advice were welcome and helped me compete better. Send-aways have always been my biggest problem. A send-away is where the dog is sent forward across the ring alone to a marked area, usually a space about four feet square. Once the dog reaches the box, the handler must give the "Down" command. My problem was I couldn't see if my dog had got to the send-away box. It was solved by teaching Katy that when she got to a send-away box she should lie down whether I gave her a command or not. I also found it difficult to point my dog in the right direction. I have had comments from judges in the past about spending too much time in the bar after sending my dog in the wrong direction. Margaret made a point of being at the ringside for me. "I will stand here. If you make sure you are in line with me you will be facing the right direction."

Ironically, Margaret discovered that one of her dogs was blind in one eye and partially sighted in the other and I was able to help her with him. Dudley would stop dead in the ring and Margaret could not understand why. On inspection, I could enlighten her. Maybe a shadow fell across the ring at that point, or there was a change in the ground colour. Margaret's dog loved working at the shows, despite his lack of sight, but to ensure nothing worried him in the ring Margaret would ask me to look at the area first and point out any part that might appear odd to me and her dog.

After my eye operation, I had to learn how to distinguish everything around me. Changes of texture or colour were confusing. I would often mistake a shadow on the ground for some obstacle and walk round it. Over the years I have learnt how to interpret what I see, although there are still times when I get caught out. Having Denis and Margaret help at the training sessions was a great comfort. "You will be fine in the big ring," Margaret assured me. "It is well lit and, of course, there are no ropes to walk into. The barriers are white so you won't have any trouble seeing those." Denis took me through the training, pointing out any little mistakes I was making.

"Keep your left shoulder back. Pip thinks you are turning right all the time."

I have never owned such a perceptive dog. A twitch of my shoulder or hand and Pip would be doing a turn without me. At one point during the heel-work training, I spotted something dark on the ground in front of me. Instinctively I jumped over it and Pip, keeping to his position at my left-hand side, jumped too. Denis became hysterical with laughter.

"That was a damp patch on the floor, but I must say you both jumped it superbly." I hoped there would be no damp patches in the Crufts ring.

The people-training came next. We all received instructions on the order we were to work. "There is a parade of dogs and handlers at the start of the day," Roy informed us. "You will follow on from the Southern team. Walk round the ring with your dogs and don't forget to smile. Everyone will be watching you; look as if you are enjoying yourselves."

Each team was given a specific colour and the Midlands was brown. I had to find brown shoes and brown trousers; the jumpers, with the Crufts logo, were provided. In 1989 brown was definitely out as far as the fashion scene was concerned. After combing every shop for miles I managed to find a pair of tan shoes, but no brown trousers. In desperation I bought a pair of grey ones and dyed them. The week before Crufts, I was kitted out and as ready as I would ever be. My Crufts bag was packed for every eventuality – safety pins, spare dog-collar and lead, dog bowl, headache pills, et cetera.

I managed to cover every eventuality bar one, and that I could not control. Pip is dominant aggressive towards other dogs, which means if a dog encroaches on his territory he will bite it. Under normal circumstances I have no problem dealing with this aggression. Pip will not go near strange dogs and if they approach him and become a nuisance, I give Pip his ball. Nothing the other dog then does would induce Pip to drop his ball and, while he has a ball in his mouth, he can't bite.

If a dog has behaviour traits, such as dominant aggression, it can be controlled but never cured. You can't change a dog's temperament. In the wild, dominant aggression is a sign of pack leadership. Every pack needs to be structured to work and survive. There will always be a male pack leader whose job it is to maintain order among the subordinates and keep away strange dogs from other packs. A dominant aggressive dog will not want to fight or be aggressive for no reason and if pack law is broken by subordinate members the pack leader will give the offending dog a quick bite to put him in his place. He will do the same with an intruder. One quick bite is usually enough. Fights only occur when the offending dog will not submit. So dominant aggression is an essential part of some dogs' make-up. It can be a nuisance, but if the owners of such dogs understand the problem there need never be any cause for worry, except that I knew tying Pip up on a bench would be a problem as far as his aggression was concerned. Give a dog an area, tie him to it and, naturally, the dog becomes aggressive to intruders. I planned for this by organising friends to sit with him at the times I would be absent.

I don't think I have ever been so nervous about anything in my life as I was about appearing at Crufts. I enjoy winning at shows. It is a satisfying feeling to be the best, but far more important than the prize is the enjoyment I get from working with Pip. With Crufts approaching, I was afraid he would pick up my anxiety and begin to worry. It can be a fine line between pleasure or pressure when training a dog. One moment of panic on my part while teaching him could blow our whole relationship. As the time drew near I wanted to back out, so bad were my nerves becoming. The day before the show I was very ill. I felt sick, had a blinding headache and the thought of food was intolerable. Pip, of course, knew nothing of his debut, so he took everything calmly, even when he was disturbed from his sleep at three thirty in the morning to get on the coach for London.

I had organised the coach myself. I felt safer that way. I could dictate the departure time to be sure of reaching Earl's Court in plenty of time. The other passengers were going to spectate and Pip was the only dog on the bus. I had asked the coach company if he could sit on a seat covered with blankets so he could travel in comfort. He thought this was really living in style, being allowed to sit up with the humans. He decided that, given this privilege, he was obviously meant to guard the bus. All the passengers received a low warning growl as they passed our seat but once on the bus they were accepted by him as friends.

When I sat down on the coach I felt wretched. I hadn't slept or eaten for over twenty-four hours and the thought of going in to the big ring made my stomach turn right over. I tried to get some sleep as we travelled down the M1 and I must have dozed off at some point with my arms wrapped around Pip and my head resting on his shoulder.

"We are nearly there." Rosemary was shaking me gently.

When I awoke, my body and brain had revitalised. I felt as fresh as a daisy and there wasn't a nerve in my body. It is a proven medical fact that stroking a dog reduces the heart rate and gives a feeling of calm, well-being. Sleeping with my arms wrapped around Pip had worked wonders. I walked into Earl's Court with great pride and confidence.

Once we had settled in, I tested Pip to see if he would work in this unfamiliar place. I found a quiet corner and ran through our test. Pip was with me every bit of the way and very pleased when I produced his ball as the reward.

At eight a.m. the team received a pep-talk from Roy.

"We are due in the ring at eight forty-five for the parade. Don't forget to look confident and smile. Show them the Midlands team is the best. While you are walking round the ring, make the most of it. Your dogs all have to work there so take this parade as an opportunity to make a fuss of them. Let them think it's a great place to be. Oh, and remember that your dogs need to spend a penny before you go in the ring."

There were areas filled with sawdust inside the building

but there was no way Pip would attend to his toiletries indoors. We found somewhere just outside but Pip would not comply. Other dogs had been there first. He wanted a fresh spot. For fifteen minutes I walked him up and down a small side street, armed with my scoop, begging him to get on with it. Eight thirty and he still hadn't. I wondered if lifting my leg up a post would do the trick – well, I was getting desperate. I had six minutes to get back and in to the ring for the parade. Then Pip spotted a dog walking past the end of the road. That did it: he marked his territory instantly.

Pip and I stood outside the brightly lit ring watching the dog before us go through his paces and my mind suddenly slipped back ten years. In 1979 Emma and I had stood here waiting our turn in the personality parade. She had been so calm about the whole affair. She had strolled around the ring, surrounded by dogs and people, without a care in the world. I looked down, almost expecting to see Emma's soft, brown eyes looking up at me. Pip had a puzzled look on his face as his almost black eyes caught mine. His ears flicked forward and the end of his tail began to wag. He must have picked up my moment of sadness, for he gave a little jump and squeak. Any nerves I had totally disappeared. I knew Pip would do his best for me.

As we stepped in to the big ring a cheer went up from the crowd. Pip stared around in astonishment at the people watching, but it did not put him off. He stretched up to his full height, his tail stood erect and he bounced joyously around the ring. He completed each exercise with great enthusiasm – too much enthusiasm. In the recall, he was left at one end of the big ring. I had to walk to the far end and call him to me. In this exercise, the dog should come and sit in front of his owner. I called Pip extra loudly, with urgency in my voice because I was afraid he would not hear me over the noise and distraction going on around him. He heard me. He set off at a flat-out gallop. I stood transfixed, watching as he approached like a greyhound after a hare. There was no way he could stop in time and I was convinced he would hit me with such force I would land in the next ring. I heard the audience gasp as he approached, but I was unable to move. I was rooted to the spot. At the last second, he swerved and missed me by half an inch. He screeched to a halt somewhere behind me. With the speed of light he was back and sitting in front of me, a big grin on his face. "You called. I came as fast as I could."

I think that performance made everyone's day. It might not have been the perfect recall, but boy was Pip keen to get to me. The whole audience sighed and then laughed. Even the judge had a smile. That mistake cost valuable points but I didn't care. Pip had enjoyed himself and that was worth more than a million red rosettes.

Back at the benches, the rest of the team wanted to know how many points I had lost. We had dropped eight – far too many, but never mind. I had completed the main part of the work but we still had "stays" to do in the ring. All the dogs from each region would do the stays together and then the marks would be totted up. Each region had six representatives and, at the end of the day, the region dropping the least points would be the winners. We weren't doing too badly but stays could change the marks drastically. Pip had to do a one-minute sit and then a two-minute down-stay. The competitors were instructed to leave their dogs, walk across the ring and keep their backs to their dogs. That is when my nerves came back. I stood facing away from Pip, praying he would not move. Two minutes seemed like a lifetime. Pip stayed exactly where I had left him, much to my relief.

Back at the benches, we congratulated each other on fulfilling the stay exercise. Now I could visit the ladies' and find a drinks stall. I warned the owners on either side of Pip's bench that he was not friendly towards other dogs. On one side there was a miniature poodle and on the other a big soft German Shepherd called Oliver.

"He wouldn't hurt a fly," his owner assured me.

"No, but Pip would and I would hate anything to happen to upset another dog."

I secured Pip to his bench, making sure he could not reach round to either side. The volunteer dog-sitter was instructed to sit in front of him until I came back. Relieved and refreshed, I returned to the benches. My dog-sitter was still there, but looking worried.

"What's the matter?" I asked as I approached.

"I am sorry, but Pip bit Oliver. I don't know how he managed to do it except that Oliver put his head round the bench and Pip snapped at his ear."

Poor Oliver had to have his ear stitched. I felt dreadfully upset. He was a good-natured dog and, luckily for me, his owner took after him. Pip had not been able to reach Oliver but the Shepherd had been able to reach round to Pip and get bitten for his trouble. It did rather mar the day for me but, checking on Oliver later, he was not worried by the event and he still remains a big, friendly, trusting dog.

Apart from the odd dashing off for necessities I stayed with Pip to ensure he behaved himself. Sitting on the bench, watching the hundreds of visitors pass, was an entertainment in itself. Most people stopped to ask what breed Pip was. All dogs at Crufts must be pedigree, I was told more than once when I confessed Pip was a crossbreed. After a few of these remarks I decided to say, "This dog is a very unusual breed, the only one of its kind here today – a Coliador." That pleased everyone and some people came back with friends to point out this new Coliador.

The Midlands team came third. The Southern team had pulled out all the stops and beaten us all. Never mind, there's always next year.

At five p.m. I was exhausted and looking forward to the

comfort of the coach. Pip was very much awake and alert. He had been resting most of the day. He greeted the cold February air with delight as we left Earl's Court. Hundreds of coaches crowded the tiny parking area.

"Where's ours?" I asked Rosemary.

"We have to meet it outside on the road. The driver wasn't allowed in here without a pass."

We piled out on to the pavement and waited. Pip might have enjoyed the fresh air but *we* certainly didn't. I was frozen by the time the cheer went up and our coach came into sight. We picked up our bags and watched in stunned amazement as the bus sailed straight past.

"Didn't he see us?" I said, turning to Rosemary.

"Well, he waved as he passed."

Another freezing ten minutes went by before the coach approached again. For a second time we grabbed our bags, but it sailed past once more. By this time our fellow passengers were not amused.

"I think he's trying to tell us something. He seemed to be waving us forward. Stay here and I'll try to follow him."

Rosemary left us at a trot and we watched as she disappeared round the corner.

"I managed to catch him," Rosemary gasped on her return. "He's waiting at a bus stop down there."

"What's he doing?"

"The police are on duty and they won't let him pick us up here. We have to go to the bus stop up the road."

We dragged ourselves and our bags up the road to be met by a very belligerent policeman.

"Your coach is not allowed to stop and pick up here," he said. "It can only stop here until a bus comes."

"Then what happens?"

"Then what happens "– the policeman stared at me – "is that your coach goes away and does not come back till I say so."

I dared not make any comment after that. I was afraid of blowing our chances of getting out of London. It took two goes to load us on because a bus came when only half our passengers had reached their seats. The M1 was greeted by all as safety, out of London chaos and on our way back to the sanity of the Midlands.

CHAPTER 6

While I was enjoying myself at Crufts, Graham lay in a hospital bed. I was worrying about him but at least he was being cared for and, at last, they would be sorting the problem out for him. Over Christmas, Graham had complained about backache and, after some weeks of visiting the doctor, he had been referred to the orthopaedic hospital. His symptoms seemed to indicate a spinal problem, such as a slipped disc.

Graham had no vices, unlike me. He never smoked and only took the odd glass of wine and he kept physically fit, riding his bicycle every day. As a piano tuner, he travelled all over the city and probably biked about thirty-odd miles each day. Back trouble seemed to fit his lifestyle. He was tall and slim and hunching over a bike hour after hour pointed to a slipped disc.

A bachelor, with his own house, self-employed, he seemed to have a good life. On the surface, I don't suppose we were very close. Weeks could pass by without us seeing each other. Sometimes when he was working in the area he would call in for lunch. Graham really loved his food, so I tried to put on a meal I knew he would enjoy. As children, though, we were very close. I am sure we must have argued, but I don't remember that. I regarded Graham as my protector.

In fact, one of my earliest recollections was of wanting Graham in preference to anyone else. We had gone to Skegness for the day and somehow I had been separated from mum, dad and Graham and ended up in the lost children's home. I remember sitting crying and the only thing I could say was that I wanted Graham.

Graham and I were like chalk and cheese, we were so different in character. He was the silent type, never one to boast about his own accomplishments and he hated the limelight. In many ways he should have had a bit of my bravado. He was a brilliant guitarist and he could have made a name for himself, being good both with popular and classical music. He was offered contracts from popular groups but, no, he was happy to keep his playing as a hobby. I would most definitely have benefited from some of Graham's intelligence. He was good at spelling and maths, and he was very considerate. Looking after a kid sister must have been humiliating for him, especially when his friends used to pass us by on the way to school and tease him. "Lumbered with her again, Graham," they would say.

The week after Crufts Show, we discovered that Graham's problem was cancer. We were all told, including Graham, that there was very little chance of survival. They did operate, which gave us a vestige of hope, but soon after we were told that there was nothing more they could do. Living with that knowledge was soul-destroying for me. What must it have been like for Graham? Mum and dad looked after him at home. I don't know how they coped but with the help of nurses who came in three or four times a day they managed. I was always afraid, when Don and I went to see him, that I would break down and cry in front of him. The thought that he knew he would not be sharing the rest of our lives was unbearable.

I remember visiting him on Saturday evening and he was waiting for *Columbo* to come on television. It wasn't scheduled that Saturday. It had been replaced by the Eurovision Song

Contest and Graham was upset and annoyed. At the time, I didn't give it much thought but afterwards I realised what it had meant to him. He didn't know how many days he had left.

His death was devastating and I don't think I will ever be able to accept the fact that I don't have a big brother any more, but the most difficult thing is coming to terms with the knowledge that Graham knew he was going to die. The thought of what he must have suffered mentally in his last few months of life will haunt me for the rest of my life.

CHAPTER 7

I feel very fortunate to have Don and Kerensa and the dogs, who all need care and love. No matter what devastating feelings I bottled up inside me over Graham's death I had to carry on. I find the dogs help enormously because they take so much time and effort to look after. Feeding seven dogs, for example, resembles a military operation. Psyche, Mocha and Katy are fed in the dog room, Bracken and Pip in the kitchen. Buttons and Teak, being the greediest, are fed outside. Buttons would steal anyone's food if she thought she could get away with it. She doesn't put her nose into the bowl, she just grabs the bowl and runs off with it. I have seen her do this to poor Mocha. Buttons snatched the bowl from under Mocha's nose and ran in to the garden with it. Mocha stared at the empty spot between her paws in total bewilderment then, thinking she must have finished her meal, she sauntered into the hall and lay down.

The dogs are let out into the garden at three p.m. and dinner is served at three thirty. They are quite happy to potter about for half an hour but the minute they hear the bowls being filled all hell breaks loose. The back door vibrates with body launches from Buttons. Teak shrieks like an out-of-tune violin. Pip puts his front paws up on the glass pane and twiddles at the door handle. He can easily open the door by depressing the handle – something none of the others has fathomed out so far – but he knows if he does open the door I will be cross with him. If he ever gets beyond himself with excitement and pushes the handle down, the door swings open and the other six dogs think I have given the invitation to enter, so they rush in like a herd of stampeding cattle. Pip, knowing the true facts, stops outside looking sheepish.

The other day Don was on the receiving end of my annoyance over the door. I was doling the food out in the dog room. I had heard Pip depressing the handle to try and hurry the proceedings along, when the door opened. "Get out, you horrible dog," I snapped. I used the singular because I knew it would be Buttons who barged through first. "How many times do I have to tell you? Wait outside until I let you in."

Don put his head round the dog room door. "Permission to enter, ma'am? I only want to put the kettle on for a cuppa."

"Permission granted," I told him with a grin.

It is imperative that, in a pack of dogs, each individual dog knows his or her name. It would be pointless my giving commands if the dogs did not know who was to comply. When the dogs are let in and out they are given their orders by name. In the morning, when Don is ready to take them for their walk round the woods, I open the dog room door and call them out individually. Teak has to be the last out otherwise she causes chaos in the hall. Being the most dominant of the dogs, she would lurk in the hall to do a rugby tackle on anyone who tried to pass her to get to the car if she was let out first. They come out in reverse dominance order. Psyche, being the most submissive, goes first, followed by Katy, then Pip and, lastly, Teak. Bracken is never put in the dog room so he always gets in the car first. Buttons and Mocha no longer go on the morning walks. They are both too old to keep up with the rest of the dogs.

I wish now I had not had so many dogs close together in years, for several of them are ageing at the same time. Bracken and Teak are both grey around the muzzle and eyebrows. Teak is still quite fit, but Bracken ails with his arthritic hip and a cataract on one eye. I feel sad now when I look at Bracken. He has had to give up his job as the PR dog since he could not manage stairs and slippery floors. His place has been taken by Psyche, who loves people and enjoys learning tricks. I am beginning to think Buttons has gone deaf, as of late she is not responding to her name. It could be cussedness, but I don't think so. She only manages to take her four legs about with her after great effort and lumbers from place to place like a hippo. As a youngster she could be quite aggressive when people came to the house, but that's diminished and all she has left is her bark. I thought she was losing that a couple of years ago. She started with an intermittent cough which gradually became more frequent. I took her to the vet for an examination. He checked her heart then delved straight into her mouth before I could warn him of the risk he was running; not from being bitten – a far worse fate than that. I would not touch Buttons' mouth with a barge pole because I know what goes into the big brown orifice. Even on the way into the vet's surgery, she had snatched something off the pavement that resembled a half-eaten fish, green with age.

"My God, it smells in here," the vet gasped, drawing back his hand.

Buttons delights in eating nasty things, the nastier the better. That very morning, she had devoured numerous rabbit droppings and a pat of cow dung. The day before she had found a dead bird smothered in maggots. It had slipped down her throat before I could scream, "*LEAVE!*" No matter how hard I try, Buttons' eating habits cannot be curbed. Her breath is like gas from a cesspit, a great deterrent if she were to breathe on a burglar. The vet stood holding his hand at arm's length. I tried to stifle a giggle.

"Why didn't you warn me?" he accused.

"I would have done, but you were too quick."

The vet soaked his hand in neat Dettol before donning rubber gloves. He tried to peer into Buttons' open jaws from a distance. "Can't see anything wrong in there."

"Are you sure? Have you looked at the back of her throat?"

"Mmm," he mumbled. "I'll give you some cough medicine for her. It might do the trick. If not, bring her back next Thursday. That's my day off."

"Coward," I said as I took the bottle of medicine and departed.

Buttons' cough didn't improve with the medicine. In fact, no amount of pills and potions made the slightest difference but after a year it disappeared of its own accord. The cough in itself did not seem to worry Buttons but it was an embarrassment. If I was walking along with her when she stopped to cough, she sounded like a tramp with bronchitis and everyone would turn and stare at me.

One day I found a large brown medicine bottle on the draining board and wondered where it had come from. I unscrewed the top and sniffed. The odour leapt up my nose and down into my lungs with a searing rapidity. Whatever it was, it seemed lethal and I screwed the top firmly back on. When Don came in for his dinner I asked him if he knew anything about the bottle.

"Oh yes, I meant to tell you. A patient brought it for me. She said it's an old-fashioned remedy for coughs."

"Why did she bring it for you?"

"When she came on her last appointment, Buttons was in the garden coughing. I went into the surgery and this patient thought it was me. She advised me to give up smoking before it was too late and promised to bring me this."

He picked up the bottle and began unscrewing the top.

"Don't do that," I warned, "it will burn the skin off the inside of your nose."

"That bad, eh? Well, give it to Buttons then."

"If I did, that would certainly get rid of her cough for her. Probably get rid of her lungs as well." I poured the lethal brown liquid down the drain. Buttons is a fool to herself, but she was just about to learn a lesson she would not forget in a hurry. She watched as I emptied the bottle down the sink and then rushed outside to the open drain. I have never come across a dog so greedy. She thought something tasty was going down the sink and, not to miss a trick, she thought she would catch it as it came out of the waste pipe. I knew exactly what she was planning so I crept outside and watched. She got her tongue round the pipe as the liquid came pouring through. She slurped greedily and then leapt up with a howl and ran round in a frenzied circle backwards. She was desperately trying to get away from her mouth.

All our Labradors are disgusting in their eating habits. The older and smellier the morsel the better. Pip is the only one who will not eat rubbish. The Labradors, and Teak for that matter, don't even stop to sniff an offered titbit, they just grab and swallow. Pip is very choosy, something I find laudable. Kerensa, who has been brought up with Labrador greed, thinks Pip is too choosy. The other night she offered him the crust off her sandwich. Like most mothers, I feel crusts are good for children, but Kerensa sneaks hers to the dogs and then gives me her clean plate. But she got caught out when Pip refused to eat her crusts. She was so astonished, she called him a "miserable dog". That alerted me to what was going on.

"So that's what you do with your crusts, Kerensa, and here's me thinking you eat them up when all the time you are giving them to the dogs."

A little later that evening, I heard Kerensa giving Pip a lecture. "If I offer you something, you eat it like the rest of them."

I don't think that cut any ice. Pip still turns his nose up at most food, unless he thinks Rahni wants it. Rahni, our one remaining Siamese cat, at the age of thirteen-and-a-half is still quite fit and healthy. Amazing, really, when you consider Pip's aversion to her. My other Siamese were convinced they were dogs. They slept and ate with the dogs and there was never any sign of animosity between them. Rahni is different. She is not a sociable animal and, although she sleeps in the dog room, her box is on the shelf, well out of Pip's reach. The other dogs don't like Rahni but they would not do her any harm and, really, Pip would be the same if Rahni hadn't bitten his ear. She was on my knee one evening when Pip sauntered up and sniffed around her whisker pads, taking in the aroma of her last meal. Rahni took exception to this big, black nose jabbing at her mouth and, as Pip turned away, she shot out and grabbed his ear with her teeth. If I had not intervened Rahni would have been "a gonner", for Pip turned instantly, teeth bared, intent on finishing her off. I just managed to snatch her from his jaws before they snapped to. From that day, Pip has hated Rahni. I often see him "sheeping" her, circling her like a sheepdog herding a flock. "Pip, leave!" is quite enough to stop him. He looks at me as if butter wouldn't melt in his mouth and then fawns around me, licking my hand in a show of submission. It is nice to allow a dog to lick my hand. I will not let Buttons lick me, although there has been the odd occasion when she has got one in before I could stop her. Normally, when I see her coming with that evil glint in her eye, I hide my hands behind my back and cover any exposed piece of flesh. The other evening she caught me unawares. I was engrossed in the television when she crept up on me. Before I could stop her, she had given me a slobbering swill across the face. My initial reaction was to scream, but that meant opening my mouth and I dared not do that for fear that some saliva might get in. I didn't dare open my eyes either. I leapt up and ran to the kitchen where I felt around in the cupboard for the bottle of disinfectant and scrubbed my face with the pan scourer.

1 Showing Pip the new Dog Control notice in the park

2 Psyche shutting the door

3 Katy always walks behind me now that she can't see

4a Pip playing his favourite game, Tug

4b Pip racing to me on the "A" recall

CHAPTER 8

I love taking dog training classes. Locally there is only so much scope and I felt if I could spread my net wider it would help my income, even if the earnings only covered the cost of feeding the dogs. I contacted the local education authorities dealing with adult education and offered my services. The Arnold and Carlton College were interested in running a class on Friday evenings. It was quite a journey from here but they were paying good money and at that time I could not afford to turn it down. When the class started in September it was still light as I crossed the city, getting from the bus station into the square to catch the bus out to the college; but as the nights drew in I began to dread the journey more and more.

I would never travel alone through Nottingham, especially in the dark, so I took Katy with me. She didn't mind the bus journeys or the hustle and bustle. It's strange how the city never posed a threat to me when I had Emma. I suppose it was because I left it all to her, and although I was aware of the noise around me it never seemed as frightening as actually seeing the people hurrying along the pavements and the heavy traffic clogging the roads. Katy looked forward to her Friday nights out. She wasn't interested in meeting the other dogs on the course so much as what she could scrounge on the way. Until I began these Friday night journeys I had no idea of the state of the city buses, especially the upper deck. Empty drinks cans and papers covered the floor. Katy had a whale of a time sorting through the empty wrappers in case anyone had dropped a sweet.

At the class she managed to convince the other dog owners she was deprived, and titbits dropped into her mouth like rain. I would leave her sitting by my bag, as I instructed, but she only had to hear a familiar command such as "Come" or "Fetch" and she would rush out and demonstrate to the beginner dogs how it was done. Once Katy has visited a place and likes it, she is keen to get there and pulls slightly on the lead. This was ideal for me. It gave me confidence. My sight is not much use in the dark and although Katy has no aspirations to be a guide dog she is not stupid enough to walk into something or jump down a hole, so as long as I followed directly behind I felt safe.

I was fully aware of the fact that Katy was developing a cataract on one eye. It didn't seem to bother her and I knew nothing could be done until the cataract had become very thick. What I didn't know was that she had a cataract developing on her other eye. I came out of the bus station one Friday evening to walk along Mansfield Road. Katy was in the lead, as usual. I felt sure we had turned left too quickly, but Katy knew the way as well as I did so I just followed. A few yards further on and I knew we had made the wrong turn as there was no traffic moving on my right hand side. Mansfield Road would be full of traffic at that time of night. Then I heard a car coming up behind us on our left, pipping its horn. I moved pretty sharply. For a good four or five minutes I could not work out where we were and then I heard a car start up above me. We were in the multistorey car park adjoining the bus station. Now that did frighten me. There I was, in the darkness in the big

66

city and Katy was proving to be of no help whatsoever. I found my way out very slowly and carefully. I was absolutely petrified.

For years I have suffered the same nightmare of being stranded in the city with no one to help me. I always wake up in a cold sweat and pray it will never happen – and here it was, my worst fear. The coward in me wanted to turn back and go home, but I have another side in my makeup that will never let me admit defeat so I soldiered on. On the main road Katy seemed to take charge again. She could see where she was going, probably because of the street lights. On a quiet road the street lights are a good guide to me, but in town, when cars pass continually with their headlights on, I get confused. Katy suddenly stopped – and so did I. I peered into the darkness, but I couldn't make anything out. I was afraid to go forward so I walked first to the left and then the right, trying to discover why Katy would not go on. I thought I could see something across the pavement but it might have been a trick of the light. Whatever it was, I wasn't risking going forward.

"Ay up, mi duck," (that's a typical Nottinghamshire greeting) " . . . you can't get round there, the pavement's up."

Bless that man, whoever he was. He put a hand on my arm. "Where yer goin'? I'll teck yer."

"Thank you. I need to get on to Parliament Street."

"Good dog you got there, mi duck, but she couldn't work out to get yer round that un."

I wanted to laugh. If only he knew. Poor Katy was as confused as I was and this kind fellow thought she was a guide-dog. I wasn't going to put him right.

"Now then, will yer dog teck yer from 'ere?"

"Yes. Thank you very much."

I made it to the training class, but what a trial it had been and I wondered what had gone wrong with Katy. It occurred to me that it must be her cataract, but even so she had one good eye. I began to observe her more closely and realised she couldn't see the rubber ring any more. She would look expectant as the toy was thrown and then a puzzled look would crinkle up her nose and her eyebrows would take on a furrowed frown as though asking, "Where did that go?" She would get annoyed if one of the other dogs managed to retrieve the ring when she had no idea where it had disappeared to. Once she got into a chase with Psyche and Pip and as she dashed after her offspring she ran smack into a tree. She didn't do herself any damage, thank goodness, but there was no longer any doubt in my mind. The vet confirmed that she was developing a cataract in her other eye and referred me to a canine eye specialist at the Newmarket Veterinary College.

It seems to me a cruel quirk of fate that not only my family should suffer from eye defects, but my dogs also. Katy was only seven and the thought of her living the rest of her life in blindness was abhorrent. Dogs are the same as people when it comes to old age. They get cataracts and arthritis, which is only to be expected, and an old dog doesn't want or need to run about. Katy, on the other hand, was still spritely and her lack of sight was hampering her. It was essential to make the long journey to Newmarket.

"Katy!" I called over the dog room door. She lay stretched out with her legs so stiff they looked as if they had been soaked in starch. One ear flicked in response. Pip lifted his head and fixed me with his dark brown, compelling eyes, trying to force me to take him out instead of Katy. She lay there shattered from her morning romp round the woods. "Come on, Katy, we have to go." She opened one misty eye.

"You don't really want me, do you? I've only just got comfy on this bed." Her expression said it all.

"Katy, hurry up," I told her in an urgent tone. She trundled out of the dog room and straight into the lounge. Before I could stop her she had thrown herself into an armchair. Talk about letting sleeping dogs lie. She was incredibly reluctant to give up her morning's sleep, but eventually I managed to persuade her to get in to the car, where she fell on to the back seat, gave a big sigh and fell asleep for the two-and-a-half-hour journey.

Rosemary was my driver on that trip and we spent most of the journey discussing Katy's lack of sight and how it had affected her.

"At least dogs aren't as reliant on sight as we are," I said, as much to comfort myself as her.

"No, but it must be very puzzling for a dog."

"I don't think dogs work things out like we do. It never bothered Emma when she lost her sight. Mind you, she was fifteen then and it would have been far too risky to have put her through an operation at her age."

"Do you think Katy will suffer if she has an eye operation? Isn't it a painful experience to have a cataract removed?"

"I didn't feel a thing. Most of the trouble humans have is because they worry. They are expecting things to hurt. Dogs simply accept situations. They don't worry about 'what will happen if . . .'"

One only has to see a dog recover from an operation, such as being spayed, to realise animals have a much better approach to recovery than we do. All our bitches who have been spayed – which is equivalent to having a hysterectomy – have recovered the day after the operation to such an extent that they are running about and behaving quite normally.

The Animal Health Trust Veterinary College is located just outside Newmarket, and it has a large equine research department. As we turned into the drive I suddenly felt homesick. It's a strange feeling to be homesick for some-where you have never been to before but that place stirred some memories deep within my subconscious. I wanted to stay there forever among the tranquility of the trees and green fields. Horses grazed peacefully and chickens crossed the roadway at a leisurely pace.

There were two dogs in the waiting room when we arrived, a fourteen-week-old Burmese mountain dog who was totally blind, and a little Tibetan terrier with suspected eye problems. I feel a similar tension in a vet's waiting room to that of a dentist, but there is always one big difference: owners talk to each other. In any doctor's or dentist's surgery I have ever been to there is silence, and if anything is said it is done so in a hushed whisper. There is something about being a dog owner that encourages friendliness. We sat discussing our dogs' problems like old friends. By the time we were called in to see Dr Barnett I was as concerned for those two dogs as I was for Katy. Once in the surgery, Katy was lifted on to the examination table. She stood there as good as gold, while Dr Barnett examined her eyes.

"She certainly has cataracts in both eyes, but at the moment I can't operate. They are not ready yet. Probably in another six months we will be able to remove them."

I was very disappointed. I suppose I expected him to do something there and then. I lifted Katy off the table and said I would be back in six months' time. Katy was amazed when we returned to the car. All this way to put me on a table for five minutes . . . you could have done that at home.

On the way back the conversation didn't flow so easily. I was trying to work out how I could make life comfortable for Katy. What could I do to make things easy for her? I came to the conclusion that she would find her own level. She would realise what she could and could not do.

The Friday night training classes came to an end because the caretaker complained about dogs being in the hall. I offered to clean up after the class. In fact all the owners offered to clean up as well, but this made no difference. The caretaker appealed to higher authorities, saying it was not hygienic to have dogs in a gymnasium. The college organisers were disappointed because our class had proved the most popular, and although I was relieved of the journey I was sad to say goodbye to the friends, both human and canine, I had made. Sadly, there are more and more anti-dog rules, controls on parks, etc. Not that I think dogs should be allowed in children's play areas, but as an integral part of our community dogs should be provided for. We are lucky in our area. Our local park is superb and dogs are still allowed there, with the proviso that owners clean up and use the bins provided by the council. I do hope dog owners everywhere will ensure they leave no mess. It only takes a few irresponsible ones to ruin it for the rest of us.

CHAPTER 9

I was terrified of the German Shepherd dog sitting opposite me in the lounge. Every time I so much as blinked he lunged forward, teeth snapping the air and snarling. I really don't have to do this, I told myself. I could refuse to see nervous, aggressive dogs. There are plenty of other problem dogs without inviting ones even I'm afraid of into my home.

When I have a dog like this visit me, Kerensa and Don get strict instructions not to enter the lounge. If I get bitten that's my lookout. Sabre was probably the worst dog I have ever seen. He was far more afraid of me than I was of him, but it was difficult to keep that fact in mind when he dived at me, threatening with powerful jaws.

Nervous aggression is one of the most difficult behaviour problems to cure because it takes such a lot of hard work on the part of the owners. It can be months before an improvement is seen and most dog owners come along thinking I am going to wave a magic wand, mutter a few canine words over their dog and all will be cured. I try to make the owners understand how the dog feels and why he is so aggressive towards strangers. A dog like Sabre sees strangers as a threat, he fears them greatly, so starts to show aggression to keep them away from him. I interpret this into language owners can relate to. Sabre's owners sat silently holding on tightly to their big Shepherd's lead.

"Your dog sees strangers as I would see an alien being," I told them. "Let's pretend you invite a big, green, slimy alien in, with six long tentacles. I would be petrified. Depending on my character, I would hide under the chair, scream and shout, or start threatening it in an effort to protect myself. Now what we are looking for is something that will stop me being afraid of that alien. If it stretched out a tentacle in an effort to be friendly I would become even more afraid, but if it stayed near the door without moving towards me I would begin to relax just a little. If this alien had something I wanted maybe I could be persuaded it meant me no harm. I love chocolate, but if this creature threw chocolate towards me I would not touch it. I would be afraid it may be poisonous. If it rolled out pound coins and then walked away I would think that rather good. In fact, if every time I saw one of these dreadful looking creatures it made no effort to approach me, and rolled out pound coins, then I would begin to look for it. It would have something I wanted. Relating this to Sabre, food will not work. He will not accept food from strangers and naturally he is not interested in money. The nearest thing to money is a toy."

I then went through the long process of explaining how a dog can be motivated to play with one toy, motivated so well over a period of weeks (sometimes it takes months) that this toy can then be given to strangers who call at the house. They can keep well away from the dog, offering no threat and throw the toy to the dog. Then the dog, as I would look for the alien with money, will in turn look for strangers to play with his favourite toy.

Some owners give up this long and arduous task to reform their pets, but Sabre became a lovely friendly dog. I saw him in the local park a few months later, playing with his toy and with not a care in the world.

I have taken ordinary dog training classes for many years and, like most trainers, at the beginning I was convinced that all problems could be solved by training the dog to obey commands. The difficult dogs which growled at their owners when they didn't want to obey I felt were challenging the owner. My only answer was, "Be firmer, make the dog do as you tell him." I failed to understand that these owners were afraid of their own dogs. How could anybody be afraid of their own dog?

I remember a few years ago an unfortunate owner came to me with a problem golden retriever bitch. "I can't control her. In the house she will often growl at me for no apparent reason and the other day she leapt up and bit my arm."

I assured her that training would do the trick. A few weeks' control would work miracles. The golden retriever bitch was sweet and on her first lesson with me she behaved impeccably; I could get her to do anything. "There you are," I told her owner confidently, "she only needs a little firm handling." I felt pleased with myself for proving to the owner that her dog was not difficult or schizophrenic. All anyone needed was patience and perseverance.

Every week, when the goldie's owner arrived at the class, she would tell me how difficult the dog had been. "Look at this . . . " She pushed her left hand in front of me. "She did this the other tea-time. My son dropped some bread on the floor. I tried to pick it up and she bit me. My husband said we should have her put down. She is obviously mental."

In class the dog behaved perfectly and she would do anything for me. I confess this type of problem baffled me. Why was the dog being aggressive at home and savaging her owners? The little goldie stopped attending classes after five weeks and I discovered she had been put down after attacking the son. I was very distressed and mystified but, above all, I felt responsible for the dog's death. The owner had come to me for help and I had failed miserably.

From that moment on I vowed that somehow I would find out why people had such problems and I would learn how to deal with them. I read every book I could lay my hands on, not only about dog training, for I discovered helpful information from books about wild animals, such as wolves. I attended every dog training course and canine behaviour seminar I could and I listened and thought.

Knowing what I do now, I feel even more guilty about the desperate owners who came for help and I could not give it. The little goldie bitch was dominant aggressive and I could have solved the problem.

Dominant aggression, where dogs attack their owners, is quite a simple problem to cure once I have convinced the owner that their dog is not mental or savage. These type of dogs want to lead the pack and they do not distinguish between people and dogs. Sadly, the dominant dog will often attack a child first, seeing the youngest member of the family as the most vulnerable and the first step up the ladder to pack leadership. Yet it can easily be put right by organising actions in the home to show the dog that he, or she, is at the bottom of the pack without using any form of aggression whatsoever.

I also see many nervous aggressive dogs and I think this is the most difficult behaviour problem to deal with because the dogs are terrified and this causes their aggression. They feel that if they show enough aggression strangers will back off and leave them alone – and, of course, they are right. Luckily, the owners can re-programme the dog to trust strangers. With a little effort and understanding, most problem dogs can be helped.

Nervous aggression, although normally passed on from the mother, is often exaggerated because the fond owner thinks the dog is being protective. A young woman came to join my training class one evening with a beautiful German Shepherd dog. At my approach, he began to bark.

"Oh dear, the poor dog is nervous," I commented.

"Bruce is not nervous, he's protecting me," she replied indignantly. "He won't let anyone near me, will you Bruce?"

She fondled his ears with slave-like devotion and I knew I had a problem, not with the dog but with his misguided owner. There was no way I could accept a nervous aggressive dog into a class. They frighten other dogs and owners. When people turn up with such a dog I explain why I can't let them join in and offer to help them by working out a special programme. I took this young owner to one side and, keeping well out of Bruce's teeth range, I began to explain.

"Your dog is frightened and that is why he shows aggression."

"Frightened? Rubbish! He's a big, bold fella. He's frightened of no one."

At that point I wanted to walk away and forget I had ever seen Bruce but I couldn't in all conscience do that. After all, that dog could attack some child. I wanted to scream at the stupid owner, but quietly and calmly I asked, "Did you see his mother?"

"Yes, of course I did."

"And was she friendly towards you?"

"Well, no, but the breeder said she was very protective of her litter."

This is a trap I find numerous dog owners fall into when buying a puppy. If the mother isn't totally friendly, beware: the pup could turn out to be nervous. I feel sorry for the owners of nervous dogs, especially when they tell me the breeder assured them that the mother was normally a placid, friendly dog and was only being nasty because she had a litter. This may be true in part, but a mother who shows any sign of aggression over her litter can pass this temperament on to her youngsters.

I tried hard to make Bruce's owner see what her dog was suffering, but to no avail.

"The other trainer I went to told me it was natural for Bruce to protect me." I shook my head in despair. "Can I join the class or not, then?"

"No, I'm sorry. Unless you are prepared to sort out his problem first, I can't accept you."

For one awful moment, I thought she was going to be abusive or try to set her dog on me, for she stared at me with something like hate. When she turned and walked off, I was relieved but sorry for Bruce. He would either spend the rest of his life being terrified of strangers or he would get put down.

I seethe with rage when I receive a call from an owner who has been advised by their vet to have the dog put down because of aggression. A typical plea is: "You are my last hope. My vet says the dog should be put down because it's schizophrenic." It is tempting to label dogs with mental disorders when one does not understand canine behaviour, but it makes me wild when I think how many dogs must be destroyed because they are "mental".

Another familiar story is, "We have taken our dog to classes but it hasn't done any good. In fact, the trainer made the problem much worse. He was trying to get the dog to lie down and the dog bit him. The trainer yanked our dog up on his check-chain collar and hit him on the nose. Now he is really aggressive if we so much as touch the collar and lead, and he hates men."

Sadly, there are still so-called trainers around who believe the answer to any problem is aggression when, in truth, an aggressive dog must be handled with kid gloves. It is upsetting to have your own dog bite you and many such owners call me in tears. "I don't want to put him down," they sob. "We all love him, but once a dog bites I've been told that's it. He can never be trusted again."

I receive such calls for help all too frequently. My job is made more difficult when the owners have been to other sources first, but I am usually the last stop before the vet.

Most of the time this job is very satisfying. It makes me feel as if I am doing something worthwhile, turning problem dogs into well-behaved companions. There are times when I fail and that is very distressing. Oscar was one of my failures.

CHAPTER 10

Animal Accident Rescue is a Nottingham charity that works to help any animal that has been involved in a road accident. A team of volunteers are on call twenty-four hours a day and the animals are picked up and taken to a veterinary surgeon for treatment. The survivors are taken to foster homes until permanent ones can be found. Oscar was a survivor. He had been hit by a car but, apart from a few bruises, he was not damaged. Animal Accident had managed to find him a temporary home with some university students. Pets found in this way are not given permanent homes immediately in case their owners can be traced. Far too often they can't be, or, if they can, they refuse to have the animal back.

I received a call from the charity asking if I could help with Oscar. He was behaving very badly in his temporary home, biting people, taking over the furniture and generally being very obnoxious. I waited for Oscar to arrive with some trepidation. A dog that has been abandoned and run down could have all sorts of problems and I fervently hoped I would be able to straighten him out. When I opened the door and saw Oscar it was love at first sight. He was beautiful: big and black, with dark brown eyes. As I looked at him he gave me a grin and his ears flicked back into rose petals. He was so like Pip – a cross Labrador/collie – he could have been his brother. I asked the student about the problems they were having.

"He bites anyone who goes near him, especially if he is on the furniture, and he chews things up. If we shut him in a room he nips at our ankles when we try to leave."

While the student filled me in on the details, Oscar and I sat looking at each other, the end of his tail giving a little wag every time I smiled at him. If only I had room for him, I thought. He's just my type of dog. He must have felt exactly the same way about me for, far from showing aggression, he tried desperately to please me. The poor dog was obviously confused. No doubt he had been thrown out in the first place because he was dominant and he probably tried being aggressive to his owners. This temperament, along with the accident and upheaval, made him unsure of strangers. Nothing a really good home would not put right.

I worked out a programme to enable the students to control Oscar and left instructions that, if a new home was found for him, I would talk to the potential owners first and ensure they did not make any mistakes. Oscar's grin came into my mind every time I closed my eyes, as if reminding me he was waiting. Waiting for a new home. Waiting for someone to love him. Animal Accident Rescue put advertisements in the local papers asking for a home for Oscar and I appealed through my pets' column, but no one came. I rang frequently to check on his progress and one day I was informed that the students could no longer keep him and he had gone to a dogs' home. There was no fear of him being put down, but very little likelihood of him finding a new home. Put a dog with slight nervous aggression in kennels and this will make the problem worse. Oscar would become his own worst enemy, growling at strangers who came to offer him a home. The thought of him in a kennel made me weep. I grieved for Oscar. In fact, I still do. If only I had managed to find him somewhere . . . if only I could have kept him. He was the result of an ignorant and uncaring home and it is terrible that we humans should condemn dogs like Oscar.

There are many charities and individuals who strive to help unwanted dogs and many more folk who, if they had the finance, would have kennels to house such dogs. I constantly pray that I will win a million pounds on the pools, not just to house the unwanted dogs but to run a rehabilitation centre for problem dogs, to give the ones like Oscar a second chance. With the right type of conditioning and training, hundreds of dogs could be re-homed. It could even be a viable business, as I am sure there are many would-be dog owners who would jump at the chance of owning a fully trained adult dog.

Quite a few owners ask me if I will take the dog off their hands. They make feeble excuses that they don't have time to train it, or their husband doesn't like the animal. I only wish I could, for most dogs would make someone a loving pet with a minimal amount of training. I dread to think what would have happened to Pip if he had been born elsewhere, in a home ignorant of canine behaviour. I know, without a doubt, that with the wrong owners he would have been a rogue dog. His dominant aggression would have caused him to attack his owners and nervous aggression would have developed so he probably would have attacked strangers, to say nothing of his attitude towards other dogs. And yet he is a wonderful dog to live with and train. I must admit he would be a great deterrent to intruders and he is not very keen on casual callers, such as milkmen and window cleaners, but I make sure he is safely out of the way before opening the door.

The window cleaner is a dog lover, or was until the other day. When he called, Bracken and Buttons gave him their usual greeting. Making sure Pip was out of the way, I left them to receive their fuss at the back door and went to do the vacuuming. I thought I could hear someone shouting but with the noise from the vacuum cleaner I wasn't sure. It was probably the radio in the kitchen, so I carried on regardless. It wasn't until I switched the cleaner off that I heard the calls properly.

"Help, help!" The voice was coming from the back garden. I ran through the kitchen and outside, and saw the window cleaner's ladder lying across the yard but no window cleaner. "*HELP!*" I looked up and there was the window cleaner hanging on to the bedroom window sill, his feet waving in midair. I gazed at him in astonishment.

"How did you get up there without your ladder?"

"Never mind that, put it up. I can't hang on any longer."

I quickly raised the ladder against the wall. He came down and stood rubbing his arms.

"Phew, that was a near one. I've been shouting for ages. Didn't you hear me?"

"Sorry, I was vacuuming. But how did you get there?"

"That dog did it." He pointed at Buttons, who was sitting with her back pressed against the gate, an evil grin on her face. For once it wasn't Pip's fault. "When I got up the ladder, I felt it rattling. She was doing a roll round the bottom. Suddenly, the ladder went from under me and I only just managed to grab the windowsill in time."

I gave him a cup of hot sweet tea and let him reminisce about the accidents he managed to "just miss" over the years. I wonder if you can insure against your dog rolling away the window cleaner's ladder?

I also wonder if there is a canine equivalent of Alcoholics Anonymous. I would hate you to think that Don is an alcoholic because he enjoys a pint or two. Most evenings he partakes of his liquid at home. At weekends he pops down to the local for an hour or so. He is very much a social drinker (or so he tells me) but it is very rare that he has one over the eight. Too much alcohol will only make him a little soppy.

The minute he walks in the door, I know exactly how much he has drunk "socially". Normally, his greeting is, "Hello, petal," and a quick word to the dogs. A touch too much and his greeting changes. I still get the "Hello" and a kiss, but he then turns to Teak, who becomes his "Teaky-twos". Teak looks at him out of the corners of her eyes and then flashes a quick glance in my direction offering moral support, but she accepts his attention with feminine grace. One of the off-shoots of Don's drinking habits is his fascination for home-brewed ale. He has tried them all.

First he tried brewing in large plastic bottles. He spent hours in the kitchen at it. "Peter has brewed gallons like this," he said with child-like enthusiasm. "He tells me it is nearly as good as the real thing." I knew better but I would never spoil his enjoyment by pointing out to him that, as a true connoisseur, he would be disappointed at the results. The bottles either blew up or turned cloudy. Cloudy beer, apparently, is the worst possible thing.

Next came the barrels. He came in one day with two huge white ones. "This is it, petal. I've found the answer to home brew. One of my patients has tried this method and he swears by his home brew." The barrels turned out flat beer, almost as bad as cloudy beer, I'm told.

"The lager sack," Don informed me, was "the latest technology in home drinking. Look, it says here, 'perfect lager every time'." I hated to disillusion him, so I left him to his brew. I was a little concerned about the siting of this miracle lager sack. Don had propped it up on the shelf in the dog room.

"Do you think it will be safe there?"

"Safe as houses."

"You don't think that any of the dogs will get curious and start nibbling the corners, do you?"

"No, there's only Katy who likes it and she's too small to reach."

The sack of lager had to stand for three weeks. It was very inconvenient having to work round it, but it made Don happy so I did not complain.

"Tomorrow night . . ." Don grinned at me, as he stood in the dog room. "Tomorrow night I can have my first drink."

"That will be nice." While trying not to sound disinterested, I knew from past experience that something would go wrong – and it did. Don had finished his tea and was standing near the dog room glancing through the newspapers when there came a quiet "plup" and then a noisy "whoosh". We both put our heads round the dog room door. Don is normally very calm and quietly spoken. He can stay calm in the most harassing situations, but this was different. He suddenly began yelling commands at me. "Fetch buckets . . . newspaper . . . quick, get the dogs out!"

The tap on the lager sack had popped out and lager was cascading over the shelf, down on to the dog beds and swilling round the floor. Mocha sat mystified at the chaos that broke loose around her, her tail swishing the floor helping to distribute the lager. All the other dogs, bar Katy, made a dash for the door. Katy thought it was her birthday, lager streaming from the heavens.

Poor Don was frantically trying to stop the flow, but every time he took hold of the sack it spurted out even quicker. "Petal, come here and put your hand there," he ordered. I tried stemming the flow from the hole. First it took one hand, then two. By the time I tried sitting on the emptying sack, most of the lager had escaped. "No, you're not doing it right." Don took hold of the sack and tried to catch the remainder in buckets, while I mopped the floor. Any minute I expected him to sit with his mouth open under the flow, like Katy.

No matter how many times I disinfected the dog room floor and scrubbed the beds I could still smell lager. It was like an old tap-room in there for weeks. Katy, well I don't know how much she managed to gulp down. After the floor was clean, she went round the other dogs licking their paws and tails and any part of them that had been touched with the brown liquid. It's a shame Katy isn't human for she would make Don a wonderful drinking companion.

CHAPTER 11

We are fond of regarding our dogs as humans, or rather as children in fur coats, but the canine brain is very different from that of the human and this is our stumbling block. As intelligent as we are, dogs can outsmart us at every turn. The problem we have in relating to dogs is that our standards of intelligence are entirely different and we judge all living things by our methods.

Many animal behaviour experts have tried to show how intelligent – or more to the point how stupid – dogs are by setting simple tests such as the dog depressing a lever to get food. Dogs do not fare very well in these situations and one could agree with the experts in their conclusion that dogs do not have reasoning power – that is if you didn't know better, and I know better. We humans are a visual species so our concept of life is totally different from our dogs'. They work mainly by scent, and information they receive in this way is far different from ours. I have a little knowledge and understanding of this different intellect as, when I could not see, much of my information came through smell and sound. I am afraid I, too, have reverted to the visual world and my sense of smell has diminished dramatically over the last few years. At one time I could smell out numerous shops, not only the usual smelly ones such as fish and chip shops, but I could smell a Woolworth's, or a Co-op or a W.H. Smith's, because no matter what city these shops are in they have the same smell. I don't quite know what the distinctive odours were – they could have been a certain floor polish or a brand of soap – but each shop and each chain of shops had their own very distinctive smell. Although I have lost much of this sense, I can still detect odours better than most people. I make my friends laugh when I announce rain, snow or fog. Often on the way home from a dog show I will mention the elements, even though the sky may be clear. My friends used to say, "Your nose is wrong this time, look at the sky," only to find a few miles on we hit the weather I had predicted. Now they ask me what the weather is going to be like as we set off.

If we were to set tests of intelligence for humans based on a sense of smell we would be hopeless. I can imagine the tables being turned and a dog setting up a scent trail for a human to follow. The dog would laugh heartily at our inability to do something which would be so simple for him. With this knowledge in mind, it is easy to see why we fail to communicate with our dogs and yet they are brilliant at communicating with us. How clever dogs are at getting what they want! Most of the owners who visit me with a problem dog fail to see that their pet has them well trained to jump to every whim. Without realising it, many treat their dogs far better than their spouses or children and then they wonder why the dog makes a takeover bid for pack leadership.

A husband and wife visited me with a collie cross who was becoming very dominant, not only with people but with other dogs. My first piece of advice was to have the dog castrated. The wife looked horrified.

"It's cruel to have him castrated," she said as she hugged the dog.

"Why do you think that?" She did not have to answer me for her expression of total devotion when she looked at the dog spoke volumes. No wonder the dog thought he was pack leader. A dominant dog will very cleverly watch and take note of the household affairs and, given the correct signals, he will think he is top of the pack. To a dog like this, being top of the pack means keeping order and that may necessitate showing aggression or even attacking one of the family members. But – and this is very important – the family have told the dog by their actions that he or she is the pack leader. Sadly, most owners fail to understand what they have done and then blame the dog. This is the reason many are abandoned or destroyed. The owners have created a monster and have no idea how to rectify the situation.

Boris (very aptly named) was one such dog – a Rottweiler. A huge, powerful dog, he had been given the go-ahead by his family to take over the pack and he did not need any encouragement to do so. His owner, a very attractive blond lady, was built more like a Poodle owner than a Rottweiler owner. She was slim and feminine, with no muscle to hold a giant of a dog like Boris. When she spoke to me on the telephone, I was a little puzzled.

"He drags me up to strangers in the street and then stands there growling at them."

A nervous aggressive dog would growl at strangers, but not drag his owner across the street to strangers and then stand growling. A dominant dog will normally ignore people in the street. I booked Boris in for a consultation. Now I am not frightened of dogs, but I am careful. I don't want to be attacked, especially by a Rottweiler, but I know the signs and signals to give to protect myself from attack. When Boris arrived I was careful not to look directly at him. If he was nervous aggressive this would set him off. I would be a threat to him if I stared at him. When I opened the door, Boris hurled himself into the hall. His owner literally could not hold him. She skidded across the carpet after him. I prayed silently that Boris would not be nervous aggressive. If he was, this could be my final hour. I sat down in the lounge, took up my pen and pad, determined not to look at Boris as he puffed and panted, straining on the end of the lead. His owner, Mrs Wicks, tried desperately to control him.

"He's like this all the time, trying to get to people. If they ignore him, he starts growling."

That gave me a lot of confidence, I must say. I managed to ask the first few questions and sneak a look out of the corner of my eye at Boris. His large chest was heaving as he panted, showing me a full set of teeth and powerful jaws. Then he spotted me looking. With one launch, he dragged his owner off her seat and I was buried under eight stone of Rottweiler. I have no one to blame but myself. If I will take on these problem dogs, what do I expect? A little voice in my head screamed, "I didn't think it would end under a Rottweiler," and then I realised I wasn't being attacked, not with teeth anyway, but with tongue. Boris was licking me to death.

He was very, very dominant and he wanted attention. He certainly wasn't getting it from me. I knew the minute I started obeying his demands he would start growling at me. I sat there, virtually crushed under his massive frame, while his owner managed to pull him off.

"He's not growling at you, he knows you're not afraid of him," she said.

Not afraid of him? I was petrified. Well, I had been until I realised what his problem was. I discovered that Boris slept on the bed and he objected to anyone else sleeping there. He was fed first, before the family sat down to eat their meal. If he wanted attention, he went up to anyone in the family and demanded it. The dog was treated like a king so, naturally, he thought he was king and felt he could command his subjects.

I asked Mrs Wicks what she would do if she was busy and the children wanted her attention.

"I would tell them to go away and wait till I had time," she replied.

"But if Boris comes up to you when you are busy you pet him?"

"Well, yes, I do."

I could see from her expression that the light was beginning to dawn.

"If Boris is in your chair, would you make him move?"

"No, but then Boris has his own chair."

"Do the children have their own chairs?"

"No, of course not."

A few carefully worded questions soon show how we treat our dogs and children. Mrs Wicks was beginning to open her eyes to Boris's little games for, at that point, she lost attention and again Boris launched himself at me. He could not understand why I did not react to him. I simply sat there while he slobbered over me. He pawed at my arms and washed my face. In the end, he gave up and sat staring at me with a very puzzled look on his face. I was probably the only person he had come across who did absolutely nothing – no show of fear and certainly no attention. He was mystified. Not surprising when you think that he was used to gaining attention from anyone he met. When Boris left, I had to change my clothes. I was wet through from his attentions.

"Hello, this is Boris's mum."

I find it revealing, the way owners refer to themselves as the dog's mum. Freud would no doubt have a field day explaining this syndrome. Boris's mum had rung me five times since her visit two weeks earlier. I was beginning to think I was fighting a losing battle with this case. What amazes me is that owners fail to comply with the regimen I set for the dogs, either because they do not listen or they do not think what I have told them to do is absolutely necessary.

When I first began dealing with problem dogs I was horrified to receive calls to tell me that my programme was not working until I realised that the owners were not doing exactly what I had told them.

"What's going wrong?" I asked.

"Last night he wouldn't let my husband in to the bedroom. It was awful."

"What was Boris doing upstairs, let alone in your bedroom?"

"I thought he could go upstairs after the first week. I thought you said to stop him going upstairs just for a week."

I am aware that being told what to do over a period of weeks can be very confusing, and it is easy to forget as the weeks go by, but I leave nothing to chance. Every owner who visits me has a programme typed out with weekly instructions to follow. I also offer a completely free aftercare service to encourage owners to contact me if they have problems. I certainly had told this owner to stop Boris going upstairs during the first week, and I meant forever. I can't wave a magic wand and change a nervous or aggressive dog into a meek little creature. A dominant dog like Boris needs to be kept firmly in his place at all times, otherwise he would revert to being the boss.

"Boris must *never ever* be allowed upstairs. If you start letting him back on your bed he will become very aggressive."

Boris's owner started crying. "But I love him. He has always slept on my bed and I don't think I could face life if he can't."

There are times, and this was one of them, when I feel like screaming and shouting at owners for their total stupidity. This dog could be a killer, he could badly damage an adult and, God forbid, he could kill a child. He had the power and the temperament if uncontrolled. Boris had been bought for Mrs Wicks by her husband as a guard dog, because Mr Wicks worked away from home during the week. A guard dog was what they wanted and that's what they ended up with, except that Boris was guarding *his* area from his owners who could not comprehend the pack laws that rule pet dogs.

I took a deep breath to calm myself. "Mrs Wicks," I said as gently as I could, "you have a choice. Either follow the programme to the letter or your dog will do someone a great deal of harm . . . "

I spent a good half hour on the phone explaining everything again in the smallest detail of how Boris should be controlled. Seven days passed before I heard from Mrs Wicks again.

"He's got to go," she informed me in a cold detached voice. "My husband says he's got to go. He stood at the top of the stairs last night and none of us could go to bed."

How can owners love the dog so much one minute that life without them upstairs is unthinkable and then the next moment they don't want the dog at all? Mrs Wicks had not followed the programme. She had decided it was easier to get rid of Boris.

It is not often I can find a home for problem dogs but Boris was one of the lucky ones. A friend had just lost a Rottweiler at the age of thirteen and he was prepared to take Boris on. I gave him the list of instructions for Boris to live by, just simple rules such as not being allowed upstairs, not being given titbits or affection every time he demanded them. Boris is now a sweet-tempered, very obedient dog who could be trusted to behave impeccably both at home and out in the street.

CHAPTER 12

In the "Dogs for Sale" column of our local paper there are always dozens of Rottweiler and Doberman pups on offer. How many of those pups will end up at the dogs' home or dead because the owners will be unable to control them? Each time there is media publicity about dogs attacking humans dozens of Rottweilers and Dobermans are turned out, and the pets' column lengthens with not only pups but unwanted adult dogs of these two breeds. Their crime is to be bought by the wrong type of people.

I received two disturbing telephone calls on this subject recently. The first was from a young boy of fourteen. He explained that he was having a problem with his seven-month-old Rottweiler dog, which had bitten his younger brother. I asked him if he could bring the dog over to see me, accompanied by his parents. No, that was impossible, he replied, and revealed he had no father and his mother did not like the dog.

The second call was from a young mother who informed me that her German Shepherd puppy had badly bitten her three-year-old child. Apparently this particular puppy was the third she had bought in the last year and they had all bitten the children. The other two had been sent to the dogs' home. My advice was to find the puppy a decent home and stop buying dogs. "This one cost me a hundred and fifty pounds and the others weren't cheap. I'm fed up with losing money on these dogs. Can't you stop this one biting?" I asked if the children would leave the pup alone, ignore it as much as possible. "I can't make them do that. They love him and they only want to play."

It is tempting to blame the dogs themselves for this aggression, or the breeding. I personally am inclined to blame the actual breeders for selling dogs to inappropriate homes.

From the information I gleaned about the Rottweiler, the dog could be dominant. In every litter of pups, no matter what the breed, the temperaments will vary from submissive to dominant though naturally some breeds are generally more dominant than others. This is a normal pattern, an essential pattern for dogs and wolves in the wild pack situation. There must be a dominant leader to each pack, one who keeps order amongst the subordinates. A strong, intelligent dog will be obeyed and looked up to by the pack members and to keep his position in the pack the leader sticks to various basic rules. The leader will choose a sleeping area that he and his favourite bitch claim, and if any subordinate dares to take up that area the pack leader will show his dominance by a growl and, if need be, a bite. The pack leader is mindful of the health of his pack so injuring a pack member would be counter-productive. He will not fight with them unless absolutely necessary, but he will warn first then if he is not obeyed he will bite. He also insists on eating first and takes the best of the kill for himself.

In a domestic situation the dominant dog will only become aggressive if the rest of the pack (people) make themselves subordinate to him. Owners do this quite unknowingly because they love their dogs. One of the clearest pictures of this happening is when a young couple have their first baby. The dog may have been a child substitute up until that time and the people are convinced that to keep the dog happy they must not put his nose out of joint. They tend to give the dog more privileges and attention when the baby comes, thinking of him as an older child.

From the dog's point of view, this is game, set and match to him. His misguided owners think he will be jealous of the baby, so they make sure each time the baby is fed he is given a tasty titbit. The baby must sleep in a different room while the dog is still allowed in the best one, the one where the owners sleep. The dog gets attention from his owners any time he cares to ask for it and, in fact, he is now getting more, as every time the baby needs attention the loving owner gives the dog a fuss so that he does not feel left out.

As far as the dog is concerned the new baby is subordinate to him, a lesser pack member. Consequently if the baby makes a nuisance of itself as it begins to crawl the dog has every right to put it in its place by a growl or a bite. One monster dog that the owners have created. The penalty for the dog is death. Looking at the facts in this light can we blame the dog? Certainly not: his owners must take the full blame for everything they have done. It may have been a very misguided love but what a price the dog has to pay.

The Rottweiler owned by the boy was probably making his first bid for pack leadership by attacking the youngest child.

In the case of the German Shepherd pup, the owner had told me how much her children loved the dog and played with him all the time. I don't know the full facts, but bearing in mind that two other pups had been got rid of I would assume that the children were cruel to the puppies, pulling them about and poking at them. No matter what temperament the pups were, dominant or submissive, they were obviously trying to protect themselves in the only way they knew how.

The Rottweiler and the German Shepherd's owners were at fault, but in my opinion the real blame should lie with the breeders for over-producing the wrong kind of dogs and for selling these owners the pups in the first place.

My ambition had always been to breed chocolate Labradors and I realised this with Buttons and Mocha, who each had three litters. I loved having pups around. It was hard work but fascinating. The big drawback was finding the right homes and I worried about it constantly. To ensure that each pup went to the right home I temperament-tested the litters and graded them from dominant down to submissive. I was insistent that the owner take the pup I chose and if they didn't they were turned away. I also tried to be careful in choosing the homes, and if I had any doubts about prospective buyers they would not get a pup from me. But I did make mistakes and on two occasions had pups back from homes I was convinced were ideal. One of the reasons I gave up breeding was because of this responsibility. I wish all breeders were so careful and if a few more gave up breeding to cut the dog population down the dogs would be at less risk of ending up put down or at the dogs' home.

Too many owners breed from their bitches, either to make money or because they think a bitch should have a litter. I have no idea why it is considered good for the bitch – would they also think every woman should have children? We are aware of over-population in humans so why should this not apply to dogs?

I would like to see tighter control over breeding, especially where owners jump on the band wagon. Their puppy cost two hundred pounds, they reason, and a litter will make a tidy sum with the dogs in vogue. At the moment the Doberman, German Shepherd and Rottweiler are popular, and these three breeds have suffered unmercifully from the macho owner who thinks it is a symbol of his manhood to have a large dog. I personally know of a man who bought a

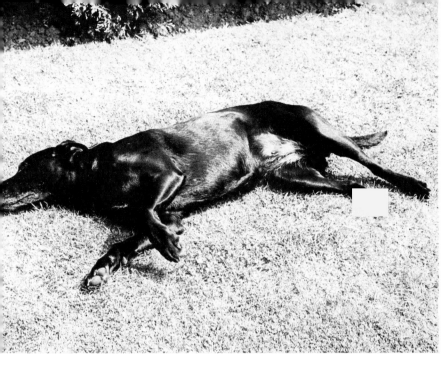

5a Psyche playing dead dog

5b Dogs waiting for their walk.
Left to right: Teak, Pip, Katy, Psyche and Bracken

6a It's a dog's life.
Left to right: Katy, Mocha and Buttons

6b Teak waiting for Don to throw the Frisbee

7a and *b* Pip and I in the ring at Crufts

8 Kerensa with Psyche

beautiful German Shepherd pup. He was aggressive to the dog, chained it up and hardly exercised it until it became aggressive. Now he is happy and the poor dog leads a miserable existence.

The aggressive dog image must be caused in part because we use dogs as guards. This, in my opinion, is barbaric and cruel. No dog should be expected to attack a human being and do man's dirty work, but while it is legal to have guard dogs then the breeding of aggressive dogs will continue. I know how guard dogs are trained. I have witnessed perfectly friendly, well-adjusted dogs turned into savage animals by people who want to make easy money. A dog which will attack anything that moves is an asset to the companies who hire it out each night to guard factory yards etc. How do they train dogs to do this? Tie them up and torment them, throw things at them and beat them with sticks. And we call ourselves a nation of dog lovers. I have also heard of establishments that sell dogs as fully trained animals, which is tantamount to giving a child a fully loaded gun. Owners buy such dogs thinking they will have a perfect guard dog, but one that will automatically know who to attack and who to be friendly with. Dogs can't work this out. Not only does an inexperienced owner have this to contend with, but he will soon find he can't control the dog because of lack of knowledge. To take on a fully trained dog it is essential that the owner knows how the dog has been trained and has had the opportunity to work with it over a number of weeks. The guide-dog is just such a case. They are not just handed over. A prospective guide-dog owner completes a month of intensive training and the same applies to the police dogs which are trained and handled by an experienced officer who is totally responsible for his dog.

I wish some control over dog ownership could be implemented. The dog licencing system did not work, and even if the fee had risen to cover the administration costs, this would only have deterred honest people from acquiring dogs. Less honest owners would have avoided paying leaving the brunt of the cost with the conscientious. There is only one sure way to stop indiscriminate breeding by avaricious people and that is for the public not to buy from them. When buying a puppy you should seek independent advice from a vet or dog training school. These are the people who will have come across dicey dog breeders and will be able to tell you the signs to look for when viewing a litter.

I often hear the blame cast on to "back street breeders", a term given by the top show-dog kennels to the pet owner who breeds. The professional dog breeders blame pet owners for defects in their breed. But some of the top show kennels are turning out dogs by the hundred with no interest in their temperament and all consideration for what the dog looks like. I see numerous nervous aggressive dogs which have been purchased from show kennels, and this is normally passed on from the mother. The owners of such dogs often tell me that the breeder did not show them the mother and had made some feeble excuse for her absence, or had claimed the bitch's ferocious barking was because she was protecting her pups.

"Why did you buy the puppy," I ask, "when you saw the mother was not friendly?" They had not thought it was important. Let's face it, there are good and bad at all levels and only the buyer can make a difference.

In the long term education will ensure better dog owners, but in the meantime I am appalled at the number of dogs at the RSPCA and wonder how anyone could buy one and then simply abandon it. I know there are genuine cases where owners become ill or die leaving their beloved pet, but what horrifies me is that the RSPCA take most of their dogs in at holiday time. The family, with cases packed, will dump the dog at the shelter and on their return from their annual holiday they will acquire another puppy. It is that simple.

The dog has suffered because of the increasing wealth in our society. In the 1950s not many families had a pedigree dog; in fact having a dog in those days, especially one with a real pedigree, was a symbol of the middle and upper classes. At the beginning of the 1960s a pedigree poodle would cost about eighteen pounds and the average working-class family could not afford that sort of money. Not, that is, until the hire-purchase system became a part of our society. One of the pet shops in Nottingham began such a scheme around the turn of the sixties and many followed suit. A good thing? I would not like to comment. On the one hand it is unfair to deny the less well off the chance of owning a pedigree puppy, but on the other a dog bought in this way made the temptation to breed and recoup the cost of purchase, plus extra cash, inviting. Whatever your views it is true that dogs are now two a penny and that must mean death to hundreds of canines.

CHAPTER 13

I felt incredibly guilty telling Bracken that he could not come with us. He had spotted the suitcase on the bed and he stood looking expectantly at me, his old tail wagging. I sat on the bed and looked him straight in the eye, his right eye. The other one had clouded over, leaving him blind on that side. Not that it bothered him. Unlike Katy, he did have one good eye so I was happy to leave well alone.

"Bracken, it isn't that I don't want to take you with us, but you are too old for this sort of thing." He suffered from arthritis in his back legs, making it difficult for him to climb stairs or get a grip on slippery floors and after much heart-searching I had retired him from the PR job he had done so well over the years. He loved going out on talks and adored showing off. Schools were his favourite outings because the children responded to him so well. Bracken offered his paw and then yawned, proving to me he still knew his tricks. I wondered how I could make him understand. He then tried giving a sharp bark and then a bow. "Oh, Bracken, I know you are a clever dog, but a long journey with two talks in two days would crease you and that would be cruel of me."

Psyche had taken over Bracken's job. She was an ideal PR dog, as she loved everyone, enjoyed learning and was active and eager to comply. I felt even more guilty when Psyche,

Katy and Pip were put in the back of the car as Bracken watched from the door. I had a talk booked in Blackpool on the Wednesday and on the Thursday I was to talk in Whitby. Don and I had decided to take a mini-break and stay with Harold and Betty for a couple of nights.

Although Betty had assented to us staying, and three dogs, I am sure she wished we hadn't been relatives. "The problem is," I told her over the phone, "we can leave Kerensa with Auntie Mu," (my long-time baby- and dog-sitter), "but to leave her with six dogs seems rather much. I have to bring Psyche with me and I don't like leaving Pip because he can be a little unpredictable and, of course, Katy sleeps with us, so I hate leaving her."

Betty gave a big sigh on the other end of the phone. "I'm sure we can accommodate you all," she said.

Not that Harold and Betty don't like dogs. On the contrary, they do and in fact Harold is as daft as a brush where dogs are concerned.

Our three snored their way to Blackpool while Don negotiated thick fog and traffic jams. Don is a very good driver, but he thinks no one else is – a sensible assumption when behind the wheel, except that he gets very aggravated. A normally placid and patient man, put a steering wheel in front of him and he grows horns. Even getting out of our drive on to the main road turns him into a seething mass.

"Where the hell do all these cars come from, just when I want to get out?" he snarls.

I have tried to make him see what is happening to his temper and told him it won't do his blood pressure any good. I have tried to make a joke about it.

"They wait for you to come out, petal. There's a line of cars parked round the corner and they wait just for you to come out and then they pounce."

I used to think banter would make him laugh and realise that getting annoyed does not help.

"Yes, they blooming well do," was his response.

Now I just sit quietly and let him get on with it. On long journeys, he gets quite beyond himself, cursing the traffic, the roads, the weather, and the journey to Blackpool was no exception. By the time we reached our destination, he was almost uncontrollable.

"This is it, get out quick. I'll pick you up at three. Be outside waiting, I don't want to get snarled up in this car park."

It was throwing it down with rain, but I did not have time to put my coat on. Don wanted to get off. He was going on to Fleetwood to take Katy and Pip on the beach. Psyche had to come with me. I leapt out of the car straight into a huge puddle. I could have become annoyed with Don hassling me, but it is no way to handle a situation like that. Instead I smiled as I glanced down at my muddy tights and soaking dress, then looked him straight in the eye and said, "I love you." He smiled, leant over and gave me a quick kiss. The one important thing I have learned while dealing with dogs is that aggression causes aggression and it does not do any one any good.

At three, I was there waiting for him. It was still raining. I desperately wanted to get some Blackpool rock for Kerensa and I knew what Don's reaction would be to my asking to go to the shops. So when I got into the car I very quietly said, "I promised Kerensa I would bring her some rock back, so perhaps we could call in a shop on the way out."

"Have you seen this traffic?" He swept a hand full circle. "We'll never get out of Blackpool if you want to keep stopping."

"I only want to stop at one shop. It would be such a shame to come all this way and miss taking back some rock for a minute of our time."

Silently, he put his foot down on the accelerator and glared through the windscreen.

"There's a shop over there . . . hurry up."

Under his breath I heard him muttering about being bogged up in Blackpool for the rest of his life if I didn't get a move on. He stopped the car and I leaped out and ran across to the shop. It's not that I jump to Don's every command, I only let him think I do. In the shop, I perused and took my time choosing different flavours of Blackpool rock. Back in the car, I told Don the reason I was a long time was because there was a queue. I could not and would not live with Don if he were like that all the time, but he has a wonderful temperament except behind the wheel, and that I can just about handle.

We had another long drive across country on the M62, which took us straight into Brough. After the hassle of motorways, Brough is like another world. I felt the tranquillity of the sleepy village washing over me as we turned into Haven Avenue and I began to drool like a half-starved Labrador at the thought of Betty's cooking – good plain Yorkshire food and plenty of it.

Harold and Betty were there to meet us. As we greeted each other, the three dogs made a beeline for the door. Pip and Psyche had never been to Brough but Katy had and she remembered it well. The three dogs gave the place the once-over and then Pip and Psyche, led by Katy, attached themselves to Harold. Katy had obviously passed on the good news to the other dogs about Harold being a pushover. Betty turned her attention to the dogs.

"Well now, my babies, auntie has to get the dinner on. Uncle will look after you."

"Come on boys and girls . . ." Harold led the way through the lounge into the kitchen and three pairs of eyes watched his every move. "Uncle Harold has saved you a little something from dinner." The dogs sat mesmerised as Harold reached for a large dish in the fridge. He turned and showed me the dish crammed full of tasty morsels – pieces of meat and chopped carrots covered in gravy. "I thought they might need a little nourishment after that long journey," he said.

I knew it was pointless protesting that the dogs should not have titbits. The most sinful thing to do, when at Brough, is to refuse food. I nodded my assent and Harold shared the food out on to three plates. The dogs' eyes widened with amazement as the food was put down in front of them. After trying to lick the pattern off the plates they followed Harold back into the dining area, where they watched fixedly as he set the table for our meal.

I have never met a couple as kind-hearted and generous as Harold and Betty. As Don so aptly puts it, they are generous to a fault. Nothing is too much trouble. Everything must be available for guests . . . ample food and drink and warmth. The place was stifling. Although it was October the weather was very mild, but Betty was concerned for our well-being and she had turned the heating on full. I was roasting. Thinking it would be cold up north, I had put on cord trousers and a winter jumper, plus my vest. I knew I was getting old when I bought a pair of vests for winter. As a child, my mum was always telling me to wear one and I balked against the idea, but as the years have passed I have succumbed to the warmth of a good winter vest.

I excused myself from the table as Betty was serving out, and dived into the bathroom to shed my vest. I laid it over the side of the bath while I freshened up.

"Are you ready?" called Harold through the door. "It's all waiting."

I hurriedly dried my hands and went to take my place at the table. Katy, Psyche and Pip huddled at Harold's feet, turning away from me when I gave them a glare that said, Don't you dare beg from the table. Best steak followed by homemade apple pie with lashings of custard left me almost immovable. When Harold came in with a loaded cheeseboard I groaned silently. Harold placed the cheeseboard ceremoniously in the centre of the table and looked across at Don with a grin.

"Now then, old lad, I want you to try this cheese. Scottish smoked."

He sliced off a huge chunk and laid it on Don's plate. Harold reminds me of a Manchester terrier – sharp, distinct features, a prominent, attractive nose and sharp, bright eyes. He stood poised, watching Don intently, like a terrier waiting for a rat to jump out of a hole. His forehead creased with a touch of anxiety, as Don took the first bite and silently savoured the flavour.

"Lovely, Harold. Beautiful!"

Harold sat down, an expression of relief and satisfaction spreading over his face as he turned his attention to me.

"Sheila, which cheese would you like to try first?" He emphasised the word "first", as if he expected me to sit there all night until the cheeseboard had been emptied. I hated to tell him I could not manage another morsel. I was about to do just that when a large wedge descended on to my plate. I couldn't offend him by refusing it and I also knew I could not eat it. I busied myself cutting up the cheese and bided my time. The meal almost over, Harold began to pop in and out of the room, taking the dirty dishes away. I waited until he had disappeared into the kitchen and Betty was looking the other way and I slipped the cheese surreptitiously on to the floor. The dogs thought it was a gift from heaven. Luckily they demolished it quickly, for Harold was back at the table.

"Betty, we want a clean dishcloth. Where have you put it?"

"I think I left one out in the bathroom."

Harold had made a good start on the washing up when I got to my feet and offered to help. I had to fight to get to the washing-up bowl over protests that guests did not wash up, but Harold finally gave way. He took up the tea towel as I continued to wash the pots. It wasn't until I had completed the job that I noted the dishcloth I had been using was a funny shape – long, with two straps at one end. I wrung it out and held it up curiously. It looked very much like a vest. It couldn't be, I told myself . . . impossible. Without saying anything, I slipped into the bathroom. My vest had gone. I walked back into the kitchen and held the soggy vest up for all to see.

"Harold, did you get this . . . er . . . dishcloth off the bath?"

He stared at it for a moment and then confessed that he had. Surely it was the dishcloth that Betty had put out?

"I hate to tell you this, Harold, but we have just washed the dishes up with my vest."

The next day (vestless) we travelled up to Whitby, Harold accompanying us. Don and Harold planned a leisurely walk along the beach followed by an even more leisurely pub lunch, while Psyche and I did our stuff for the Ladies' Luncheon Club. I was delighted at Psyche's aptitude for this work. She settles calmly under the table while lunch is in progress and then she comes out to perform the few tricks she has learnt so far. She certainly throws herself body and soul into her learning – maybe a little too much. After my talk, she emerged from under the table to "speak", or bark on command. Bracken is always very calm about his work; he is a very relaxed performer, whereas Psyche gives it all she's got. For Psyche to obey the "Speak" command, she has to hurl herself off the floor into the air like a cork popping out of a champagne bottle. "Speak," I told her and she threw herself skywards. The only problem was the table was in the way. A long table, seating about eight guests, leapt into the air, throwing cutlery, cups and flower arrangements off in every direction. It was quite a relief to get back outside into the October sunshine and meet Harold and Don.

"I would like a walk down to the harbour before we leave and have a look round the shops," I said. Both faces dropped. Mention shopping to men and they recoil and invent sudden ailments.

"You and Don go. I don't fancy climbing up and down those steps and anyway Katy would find it difficult, wouldn't you, my pet?" Harold stroked Katy lovingly. Don reluctantly agreed to come with me, while Harold took Katy along the front. As he walked away I heard him talking to her.

"Now then, little girl, uncle will look after you. Mind now, there's a step coming."

I couldn't help it, I had to laugh. Now I can see, Harold is lost for someone to care for and Katy is just what he wanted to lavish his love and affection on to. Harold stopped at every step, telling Katy to be careful, and he waited patiently for her to negotiate the kerbs.

"I don't know what he will do when Katy gets her eyes done," I said to Don.

"Don't worry, he'll find some lame dog to escort around."

Don was right. Harold and Betty attract lame dogs round them like wasps to a jam jar. If I ask them to come and stay for a few days, it's, "We would love to but old Mrs Thingy relies on us for Sunday lunch," and then there's, "Mr Whatsit, he wants his shopping doing on a Friday and this week we have to take the neighbour's uncle to the station."

Despite their activities, the bungalow in Haven Avenue is tranquil and serene. I enjoy a day or two up there, but that is about all I can stand. It is too quiet and leisurely for me and I would sink into mindless oblivion given a week of such peace. Home is rather hectic. Each day is like a ride on a waltzer. At night, when I get into bed, I can still feel the whizz and whirl until I sink into sleep.

CHAPTER 14

The more I see of other breeds of dog, the more I am convinced that Labradors are the ideal family pet. I have never had a dominant aggressive Labrador to deal with. They can be quite dominant in the way they rule their owners, but aggression to humans seems very rare in the breed. However, they are not without their faults. Many male Labradors become aggressive to other dogs and there is the eating and chewing syndrome to contend with. Before I knew how to stop this wholesale destruction that most Labrador pups embark on, Bracken had just about demolished our kitchen and garden. He tore up the Cushionfloor, ate a giant-size hole in the split-level cooker cupboard, devastated the walls – which have wood panels – and ate all the rose bushes in the garden. I tried every nasty tasting substance I could think of. Hot mustard went down a treat and, in fact, it started the other dogs chewing the wood. I really thought I had cracked it when, after pasting the walls, I let the dogs into the kitchen. They smelt the mustard, gave a tentative lick and then, to a dog, they relished this extra treat and licked the walls clean.

A few years wiser and I know how to stop them, but the one problem I have never been able to cure is Teak's food thieving habits. I have tried every trap imaginable but she susses it out. The final straw was our Christmas cake last year. Don and I were laid up in bed with flu over Christmas. We managed to drag ourselves out of bed to do the necessities, but the dogs were looked after by Kerensa and Auntie Mu. The Christmas cake stood, in full glory, in the centre of the dining room table, awaiting our recovery. The dogs are not allowed in the dining room, so it is the safest place to leave food (normally), but somehow the door had been left open and Teak took her chance. We were left with a few crumbs and a plastic Santa Claus.

To say I was furious was an understatement. I really wanted to give Teak a good verbal going over to release my anger, but that would have been pointless. Once a dog has done the dirty deed, it is cruel to reprimand him. I had a better idea. I had seen something in action on a dog training seminar that would do the trick – and trick it was, too: a detonator that banged loudly once released. I purchased some detonators and caps from the Trick and Magic Company and set about curing Teak once and for all. The little detonators are placed under an object and as soon as the object is picked up, *BANG*. In the catalogue of tricks, this is depicted as a good joke to play on visitors. The detonator is placed, say, on the toilet seat. The unsuspecting visitor lifts the seat and probably has a heart attack. I am not one for practical jokes. I loathe anyone playing them on me so I would not dream of doing such a mean trick, but Teak was different. If I could cure her thieving habits by detonated food, then I would.

It worked like a charm. I put a piece of cake on the edge of the dining room table and casually left the door open. Within minutes, *BANG*, and Teak came rushing into the lounge with an astonished expression on her face. To make this method work completely, I set up food traps in various different places and caught Teak out once or twice . . . and Kerensa. I had set a trap in the kitchen. A piece of stale cheese sat innocently on the work surface waiting for a victim. Kerensa had been out when I set up the trap and on her return she went straight into the kitchen in search of food. Like many teenagers she is like a Labrador, constantly hungry. I was engrossed in a television programme and had completely forgotten the booby-trapped cheese until there was an explosion. Katy, Psyche and Pip, who had followed Kerensa into the kitchen, now came rushing into the lounge. They had big grins from ear to ear and danced about in front of me, tails wagging. I knew exactly what they were saying: Kerensa's pinched the cheese. Ha ha!

A word of warning to any owners who have thieving dogs. Unless you know what you are doing, using something like this could harm your dog's temperament. A nervous or shy dog would go to pieces given this type of treatment. If in doubt, consult a behaviour expert before trying it. Teak now gazes at food longingly with a wistful look in her eye, no doubt remembering the time when she could steal food that did not go bang. The noise has frightened her off, but not left her with any hang-ups. If she hears a bang now, she looks around to see who has dared to pinch the food.

"It has not worked," is a complaint I sometimes receive from an owner who has brought their dog to be cured. At first, a call like this would make me feel inadequate. What had I done wrong? Why hadn't the programme of control set for the dog worked? After a little more experience of dealing with dog owners, I now realise that it is the people as much as the dogs I need to use the psychology on. Getting the truth from people needs low cunning and often a lateral approach. Dogs can't tell lies. They always show their true colours.

I have discovered it is not so much the questions I ask but how I ask them that matters. For example, a simple question to assess whether the dog respects the owner enough to move for him can be phrased, "If your dog is in the way, do you make him move?" Most owners will state categorically that they do make the dog move, which I know is not true. Phrase the question in a different way and I always get the truth. "If your dog is in the way, do you walk round him or step over him?" They fall straight into this trap by agreeing, "Oh yes, I always walk round him."

We humans are strange creatures. We often give the answer we think is right, not the truth, and patience is my byword, especially when dealing with neurotic or frustrated owners. I have learnt to be very calm and tactful. Not only do I deal with the calls for problem dogs, but I also get involved with Don's patients with problem feet. When Don is out, I can spend hours on the phone with people who want to tell me about their feet. I wonder sometimes how we both manage to keep control. Both Don and I are dealing with people's problems. Most of the time I manage to run smoothly through each day without turning to the tranquilizers. Last Tuesday morning, however, came very near to total confusion. At eight thirty the phone rang.

"Help! If I have to live with this dog another day, I'll go mad. I even had the police round last night." The poor woman was on the verge of tears. "I don't want to part with him. He's such a good lad apart from the noise. The neighbours aren't speaking to me any more. If you can't help me, I don't know what I'm going to do."

"Tell me about it," I said soothingly.

The caller went on to tell me about her dog's barking and howling when left during the day and at night. "Can you see us now?" she pleaded.

I agreed to fit her in that morning and proceeded to give directions from the M1. She interrupted me. "I can't bring him to you. He goes mad in the car. He leaps about and bites anything that gets in his way, including me."

I explained that not being able to drive, I was unable to visit. At that point, she did start to cry.

"I don't want him to go. I do love him, but what can I do?"

"Put him in the back seat of your car and tie him up securely so he can't jump around."

"But what am I going to do when I get to you? If I put my hands anywhere near him when he's in the car he bites."

"You get here and we can sort that out."

At ten o'clock the doorbell rang. Obviously my noisy dog problem.

"Is this the right place for Hocken?" the woman asked. I told her it was. "He's been a real pain, cried all the way here. I kept telling him it wouldn't hurt, but you know what they are like at this age. Perhaps if you come down to the car, he might behave himself and we can get him to come in."

I picked up my anti-bark spray, a revolting-tasting liquid I use to stop dogs barking. It is quite harmless but gives the dog a nasty taste in its mouth. It is useless shouting at barking dogs. They misconstrue this, thinking the owner is joining in on the noise. With a dog that gets hyped up, the worst thing an owner can do is shout. A quick spray on the nose and then praise works wonders.

"Did you secure him in the back of the car?" I asked as we walked down the drive.

"No." She gave me a puzzled look.

"To stop him jumping about and doing any damage."

"Do you think jumping about will do some damage to it, then?"

"I thought you told me he became quite aggressive in the car."

"He can be a real pain, but I wouldn't say he was aggressive."

I am quite used to this change of attitude from owners. They suddenly become ashamed, thinking it is all their fault. My job is to convince them it is not really their doing and the dog can be cured without any raised voices. She opened the car door.

"Here's a nice lady, look, to make you better."

"I suppose he only starts when the car is moving. Perhaps we should drive round the block and then if he starts I can spray him on the nose with this." I held up the spray. She stared at me open-mouthed and as I looked into the car I discovered why. There was no raging canine in the back seat, but a little boy who looked terrified.

"I am sorry, I thought he was a dog. I mean, I thought you were the lady I was expecting with a dog."

"I didn't know you treated dogs' feet as well," she stammered.

I certainly got off on the wrong foot there. I managed to convince her that I was not the chiropodist and she would find him in the surgery at the side. I also reassured her that Don was not in the habit of spraying his patients before treating them.

A few minutes later I heard a dog howling and barking. I looked out to see a bearded collie cross racing up the drive, the gravel flying in all directions as the dog scrabbled with his paws in an effort to reach the front door. His owner was red-faced and flustered.

"I have had a job with him. I tied him up, as you suggested, but it didn't stop the noise."

Liz Calver proceeded to tell me the problems she was having with Billy. He was a beautiful looking dog, slate grey and white with sparkling brown eyes, and a real rogue if ever I saw one. Every time the dog moved his owner began to shout at him and yank at the lead, and the dog then fought all the harder to get away from her.

"He's like this at home, drives me mad he does, up and down all the time."

"Let go of his lead and ignore him for a while."

Billy hurled himself around the lounge, and when he had investigated everything he went back to his owner and began pawing at her.

"No, don't push him away and don't say anything to him."

Billy tried desperately for a few minutes to get attention and then he sat down, confused. We were silent. Billy lay down and went to sleep.

Liz looked at him in amazement. "He has never done that. At home he pesters me. What have you done to him?"

I wish every dog was so easy. I had done nothing, except understand what was causing the problem. Billy had learned that he gained attention if he was naughty, even if it was the wrong type of attention. Like a naughty child, being shouted at was better than being ignored. Liz had got into the habit of shouting at him to behave, lie down, shut up, and if he pawed and jumped at her he managed to get a reaction.

We took him for a ride in the car. The moment the engine started so did he, screaming and barking, and Liz shouting at him. Liz had tethered his lead to the dog guard but Billy was still able to rush from one side of the car to the other in rapid succession.

"Stop the car," I told Liz. I shortened Billy's lead to give him enough room to be comfortable but not enough to hurl himself from side to side. "Now when you start the car don't say anything."

As Liz turned the ignition Billy tried to launch himself to the left and then to the right, but he could not. For a moment he howled with annoyance, then as we travelled down the road he sat down with a whimper and a few yards further on he lay down quietly. Some dogs get excited in the car: the noise of the engine, passing vehicles, an owner shouting add up to the excitement. A dog has no idea what the owner is shouting at. Billy certainly did not think Liz was shouting at him to be quiet, he thought she was joining in on the noise. His biting was sheer excitement, goaded on by Liz getting excited.

I see many cases of noise or aggression that the owners actually cause by shouting at the dog. A common fault is a dog barking at passers-by in the garden. The owner gets annoyed, rushes into the garden and shouts at the dog; the dog thinks the owner is shouting at the passer-by and naturally feels he is being backed up. He barks, his owner shouts. The more agitated and aggressive the owner becomes towards the dog the more determined the dog is to see off the offending passer-by.

Much confusion is caused by dog owners who insist their dog knows every word, especially when it comes to behaviour problems. "He knew he had done wrong," is an all-too-often phrase used by an owner who thinks the dog knows it is wrong to chew up a pair of shoes. Why is it wrong? No one would tell a wolf he was wrong for chewing up something he came across in the wild. No one chastises the wolf for cocking his leg where and when he feels like it. Yet we expect our dogs not only to understand the English language but to have a conscience.

When I am trying to get owners to understand the difficulty their dog has interpreting their wishes, I put them in the place of the dog. And this is exactly as I explained a dog's view to Liz.

Pretend you are a five-year-old child in a strange country. No one speaks English. An adult takes charge of you with every good intention, and holds your hand tightly and walks you down the road. Someone is walking towards you and suddenly the adult begins to wave his arm and shout. Depending on your temperament you would either follow suit or you may be afraid – you do not understand the language, remember: it could be their way of greeting, it could be threatening. You may try to escape and run away, and then your adult becomes annoyed with you. "What have you learned from that situation?" I asked Liz.

"I would be totally confused and I can understand how I must confuse Billy when I shout. I do tend to start waving my arms about as well. I suppose I just lose my temper. I was convinced he knew what 'be quiet' meant and he made a noise to annoy me."

Dogs are clever at picking up words that go with actions, and that can often be a problem to us humans. If our dogs understand what we mean when we say "Walk" then why shouldn't they understand other words we use constantly? The answer is that we are inconsistent. When we tell the dog we are going for a walk, we pick up the collar and lead and take him out. The dog soon learns what "Walk" means because we do the same actions every time and he gets a reward. The actual walk is a reward. Now why doesn't our dog always sit down the first time we give him the command? Two reasons: he may not have been rewarded each time he complied so why should he obey? And has the command been taught correctly? Did we put the sit action with the word?

Training can be a very hit and miss affair because we think our dogs not only understand but want to obey. A well-trained dog has been shown what is expected of him and has been constantly rewarded for his efforts. I try to look at training from my dog's point of view. When I am training Pip I ask myself if he knows what I want him to do and does he want the reward? Even so I make silly mistakes. I was teaching him to sit, lie down and stand at a distance away from me, for this exercise is part of the advanced class at the obedience shows. For the purpose of the competitions the dog must obey all three commands in any order dictated by the judge, and marks are lost if the dog moves towards the handler. Most dogs naturally step forward when going from the sit to the stand. They don't understand the rules of how to win at shows. I have seen a lot of dogs doing this exercise in a very worried manner and they certainly did not look as if they were enjoying themselves, which to me is the most important thing about dog training and competitions. The dog should enjoy what he is being asked to do. There are many different methods of training this exercise in such a way as to prevent the dog moving forwards. Owners often train their dogs at the top of the stairs so they can't move forwards without stepping down.

I enjoy the challenge of how to train different exercise in such a way that Pip will enjoy doing exactly what is required in the ring. I was seeking a method of training distant control that would make him want to obey and to stay away from me. The perfect answer was the ball being placed behind him. I put his ball about a yard behind him, walked away, gave him a command to sit down or stand, and as soon as he obeyed he was given the go-ahead to fetch his ball. He adored playing this game. He would look to me for the command and then back at his ball. When I told him he could fetch the ball he would leap into the air with great delight. Everything worked perfectly until I made a silly mistake and gave him the wrong command. He anticipated the "Fetch your ball" command and to stop him I said "Wait" when I should have said "Leave". For three days he would not stand on command and it dawned on me that I had given a "Wait" command as he stood up. He is never given a "Wait" command except when he is expected to sit. I soon corrected my mistake, but one word used incorrectly had Pip in total confusion.

CHAPTER 15

I thought Rahni would be the first to go out of my Siamese cat family as she is very timid and bronchitis has troubled her from the age of four, but she soldiers on. They say creaking gates last the longest. I still miss Ming and Ohpas. Ohpas was my first Siamese and it was his superb temperament and loving nature that hooked me on to the breed. Ming came soon after and she cemented my love for the Siameses. I don't think I will ever find another Ming. She was so outgoing and lovable, with a streak of sheer devilment. Nothing escaped her notice. Many was the time she would swipe a piece of food off my fork just before it entered my mouth. As a kitten, movement of any type fascinated her. She would sit on my knee watching my face and gently paw at my eyelids. She had no fear of the dogs and she and Emma were real buddies.

I wish Rahni had the same characteristics. I bred her myself, so I can personally vouch for her parentage. Both her mother and father had superb temperaments. As a kitten, she was rather shy, quite an endearing quality in a little animal, but infuriating in an adult. Kerensa once showed Rahni her hamster. Rahni took one look and bolted in terror. Kerensa calls her "the old bag" and I can't say I blame her, for if anyone except me approaches Rahni, she spits and lays her ears back in a most threatening manner. I know she wouldn't scratch or bite (not people), but try telling someone else that the cat who looks menacing will start purring if you stroke her. I could blame Don for Rahni's lack of social prowess, but I won't. As a kitten, one glimpse of Don would send her scuttling into a hiding place. He would laugh and say, "You would think I was going to grab her and put her in a meat pie." He said this so often at the sight of Rahni's receding tail, that even now he only has to whisper "meat pie" and Rahni disappears like greased lightning.

She does not get on well with the dogs, unlike my other Siamese. Occasionally she will try to curl up next to the dogs on the settee (not Pip), but they will have none of it. When Bracken or Mocha are in the chair Rahni tries to sneak up and steal their warmth. She slowly edges her way behind the dog, but no sooner has she got comfy than she is twigged and great growling begins. It normally ends with the dogs moving out of the way. One evening Rahni misjudged the dogs, and thought the black one on my lap was Katy. It was Pip. Rahni slithered on to the arm of the settee and in no time Pip was a fierce ball of black fire. Luckily I am still fast and I grabbed him with one hand and Rahni with the other. I am beginning to think Rahni leads a charmed life but then she takes great care of herself, especially in winter. She turns into a hermit, retreating to her big box in the dog room and emerging only at meal times. She never goes out of the door from October to May, but one year she disappeared on 5 November.

I am normally careful with pets on Bonfire Night but because of Rahni's winter habits I didn't think for one moment that she would venture out. It was quite a mild day, so the door was open most of the time. At four o'clock I noticed Rahni's absence. In a panic I began to search the garden. No Rahni. I searched the house. No Rahni. She never leaves the garden . . . never. I spent the whole evening in agonised torment, thinking of the dreadful things that could have happened to her. We all searched the garden a hundred times, to no avail. At midnight I was ready for a nervous breakdown, tortured by horrific pictures of Rahni in distress. The back door was wide open in case she came back.

"There's no point us both staying up. You go to bed and I'll wait for her," Don offered.

"I couldn't sleep for thinking what might have happened," I said. "You go and I'll wait."

Don had only been gone a couple of minutes when he called down the stairs.

"Petal, come here a minute. I've got something to show you."

Grudgingly, I mounted the stairs. I thought maybe Don was trying to cheer me up, take my mind off Rahni, and nothing would do that.

I followed him into the bedroom and watched, without interest, as he lifted the quilt. Curled in a ball was Rahni. After hours of worry there she was, safe and sound, oblivious to my near breakdown. I could have throttled her, but instead, I calmly picked her up and took her downstairs, muttering to myself.

Apart from that scare, Rahni has only caused one other time of worry when I found a lump on her tummy. The vet was concerned and advised its removal quickly. I felt depressed when I took Rahni in for her operation. I could not cope with the thought that it could be cancer. I told the vet my fears and asked him to call me while she was still under the anaesthetic if he had any doubts about her survival. I still feel guilty over Shadow's death. At the time I wanted to keep her alive as long as possible, just in case. I was told nothing could be done for Shadow and that the bone cancer would spread. The vet supplied me with painkillers for her and told me to call when I felt the time was nigh. Those last few weeks of Shadow's life I kept hoping it would go away. When I look back, I feel incredibly guilty that I let her live as long as I did. It was pure selfishness on my part. I should have ended her life while it was still enjoyable to her, instead of prolonging it.

I was determined Rahni should not spend her last few weeks on earth suffering and the vet assured me that if he was in any doubt he would ring me. When no phone call had come by one o'clock I rang the vet, to be told that Rahni was perfectly all right and I could collect her. The lump had been removed and the vet felt it was nonmalignant. When Kerensa came home from school the first thing she said was, "How is Rahni?"

"She's fine," I said. "In fact, she's sitting by her bowl in the dog room waiting for her food."

"Can I give her some?" I think Kerensa felt a little guilty over the way she normally spoke about Rahni.

"Of course. There's some chicken, you can give her that."

As Kerensa approached the cat, offering the tasty morsel, Rahni let out a loud miaow, spat at Kerensa and disappeared into her box.

"I see she is still the same old bag," Kerensa commented.

Three months later the lump reappeared, plus others, and Rahni grew thinner. The vet asked me to try her on some tablets to help the kidneys function.

"These lumps are skin cancer but they will not make her suffer at the moment. The weight loss, that's a different matter. Give her a week's course and see if she picks up."

The vet I use is quite a long way from Stapleford and I was worried he would not come out.

"Just in case . . . "

"Just in case what?" he asked.

"If the tablets don't work, she will just get worse and suffer, won't she?"

He nodded.

"I won't let that happen and I'm not bringing her here to

be put to sleep. That would cause her stress. Will you come out if I need you?"

He promised he would and I prayed I would not need to call him.

After the week's treatment, Rahni showed no signs of improvement and I knew what I had to do. She was purring when the vet came and it almost broke my resolve, but then I remembered Shadow. I didn't want another animal's suffering on my conscience for the rest of my life. Rahni was fourteen, she had had a good life and to prolong it would only cause her pain. I laid her down on a blanket on her favourite chair. Buttons, Mocha and Bracken greeted the vet, then Buttons and Mocha returned to sleep the day away on the settee. Bracken came to me. He sat quietly, not asking to be stroked, occasionally looking up at me. Some dogs have this special sense and Bracken is one of them. He knew exactly how I felt and he sat there long after the vet had left, just being a comfort to me.

CHAPTER 16

Variety is the spice of life and I love it. I could not adjust to the routine of a nine to five job, although there is a lot to be said for steady employment. At least I would know where I should be from Monday to Friday – at work. Being self-employed, with such diverse activities as writing, public speaking and canine problem-solving, I never know what I will be doing or where I will be from one day to the next. There are no days off and my work does not finish at five. I would not change one bit of my life. I consider myself very lucky but things get rather hectic at times.

One Wednesday morning, we all overslept. Kerensa had to make a mad dash to school and Don and I rushed to get the dogs out. Don takes Bracken, Teak, Katy and Psyche round the woods and I take Pip to the park. Most of my friends think because I work from home I have plenty of spare time. On the contrary, there are days when I don't even get time to eat until late at night, so I always make a point of taking Pip for his walk in the morning to keep our working relationship sealed. You won't see me training him like mad in the park. Our relationship is built on play. If Pip is keen to play with his ball, then he will work for his ball. The whole point of training like this is that the dog does not actually think he is working. He thinks doing heel work or retrieves is all part of a big game to get his ball. There is absolutely no pressure put on him to work.

This year we did not qualify for Crufts simply because we were both too busy having a good time at the dog shows. Some owners take the sport far too seriously and, consequently, pressure their dogs. I want to win, of course I do, but not at the expense of my dog's pleasure. Pip could have won quite a few classes last season except he was too enthusiastic in his "A" recall. This exercise is where the owner leaves the dog in a stay and walks away. At a signal, the dog must join his owner on the left side and continue doing heel work round the ring. I encouraged Pip to come as far as possible when called by throwing his ball once he reached me. This was a lovely game, except he often got carried away and could not stop when he reached me, a fault in the ring we lost marks for but most judges smiled and told me how nice it was to see a dog enjoying his work so much. Comments like that are better than rosettes.

Once in the park with Pip in the mornings the rest of the world disappears. I become so engrossed in our games I am completely oblivious to what is happening around me. As soon as we enter the park gates Pip circles me, waiting for me to throw the ball, and the longer I make him wait the more excited he becomes. I think he would turn cartwheels if he thought they would bring the ball out of my pocket. I suddenly hurl the ball as far as I can across the park and Pip shrieks with sheer delight as he races after it. I always use a ball in a sock, for two reasons: there is no danger of it getting lodged in his throat when he leaps up to catch it, and secondly we can't play tugs with an ordinary ball. Pip loves the chase and, being dominant, he also loves tugging. He enjoys showing me how strong he is. He races back with the ball and pushes it into my hands. If I don't take up the challenge and pull he gets so frustrated that he tries to bark without letting go of the ball. The instant I take hold of the sock he throws himself backwards, paws digging into the grass, his tail held out behind him fluffing to twice its normal size. I am not sure whether he does this for balance or to make himself look bigger. However hard I tug I cannot get the ball, and when I feel my shoulders are about to be dislocated I let go. I can get him to release the ball when I want it by giving the "Leave" command, for without this control he would soon begin to believe he was better than me and make a takeover bid. With the ball back in my pocket Pip dances around grinning at me.

My morning walks are a tonic and set me up for the day ahead. An hour of sheer joy and freedom, away from the telephone and the housework, it is a very special time for me and I try not to let anything interfere with it, so when I heard a dog whistle and someone calling frantically I ignored them. The weather was appalling with gale-force winds and so the sound wasn't clear, but then Pip stopped. The calls and whistles became more frantic and I looked around to see if there was a loose dog running from its owner. The wind dropped for a second.

"Sheila, hurry up! You should be in Newark!"

It was Don's voice. I raced across the park to him.

"What do you mean I should be in Newark?"

"When I got home there she was, this headmistress who's picking you up. I wondered who on earth she was when I pulled up the drive. She emerged from the back gate as if she had been circling the house."

"Newark? That's not till tomorrow, Wednesday."

"Petal, it *is* Wednesday."

As we drove away Don grinned at me. "It must be your age. Mind you, that poor woman was beginning to think she had the wrong day. She had knocked at the front and then the back and she had even tried the surgery."

At home I was greeted by an agitated headmistress. I changed from muddy clothes at break-neck speed while she rang the school to rearrange the schedule. I felt dreadful about the confusion. I could not expect anyone to understand how easy it is to be so disorganised as to be walking the dog when I should be talking to a school, but all was not lost as the talk was moved from before playtime to after.

Psyche was excited when we got in the car and sat on the back seat, her tail drumming tattoos on the door. She absolutely adores children, even to the point of wanting to stop and talk to any we meet while out walking. I put this down to Kerensa being such a good companion to Psyche when she was a puppy. Every day when Kerensa came home from school she would play with Psyche. An old piece of knotted rope hung behind the pantry door was Psyche's favourite toy and she and Kerensa would play tugs until they were both exhausted.

Psyche was thrilled to find we were speaking to children and she bounced into the school and gave her wriggly-giggly welcome to everyone.

I could not give talks dogless. I would be terrified of standing alone in front of an audience of adults or children. A dog gives me confidence. I love speaking and it is amazing how audiences differ in their response. To some extent this depends on area. Birmingham audiences are great, and the northern ones are particularly receptive. In all the years I have been giving talks I have only had one bad audience, a mixed luncheon club in Preston. There was hardly a titter at my punch lines and however hard I tried I could not "feel" them. Within two minutes I can assess an audience and tailor my talk and change the punch lines accordingly. The better response I get the better talk I give. The joy of public speaking is being able to control an audience, to capture the people, to make them laugh or cry. The Preston crowd were a dead loss and I would only need to meet one or two more like that and I would give up public speaking. Children are always receptive because they are interested in the dog.

Psyche was really getting her act together and since she could speak on command our repertoire had grown.

At one time I felt I would never get her to bark on cue. She just did not bark, not even when the doorbell rang or in the excitement of a game, but without a barking dog tricks are limited so I was determined to get her "speaking". Anyone who thinks they can train dogs should try teaching a dog something that can't be forced. Dogs can be forced to do most things, such as walk on the lead, do recalls etc, and a trainer can use dominance and brute force to make a dog obey. The art of training is not using force but using reward and motivation. It took me ten weeks to teach Psyche to "speak". It may seem like a long time but from a dog who made no noise I was very pleased with my accomplishment. At feeding time I stood with Psyche's bowl in my hand and asked her to speak. Of course she had absolutely no idea what I meant and she would try everything she knew to get me to place her dinner on the floor. She would throw herself into a down, then a sit, then leap into the heel position. At first I could not get a squeak out of her and would give her the food after a minute or two. Often the results are nonexistent but one must still give a reward or the dog stops trying. After about a week of silence Psyche began to whine very softly as she hurled herself about trying to find out what I wanted from her. The instant she whined I gave the "Speak" command and put her bowl on the floor. As the weeks went by her whine became louder and louder and then, eureka, it was a bark.

The school hall was crammed with juniors. They sat reasonably quietly as I told them what it was like to be blind and about how Emma guided me. Their behaviour was not so much due to my enchanting lecture but the promise that Psyche would do her tricks for them at the end. She performed with great delight, showing the children how she could lie on the floor playing dead dog, roll over, give a paw, bark her age and bow. She was then allowed to mingle, her shiny black body wriggling in and out of the children in sheer ecstasy. She is the epitome of a giggly schoolgirl. After the children had returned to their class rooms I looked round for Psyche. She had disappeared. I found her in the middle of a class receiving more adoration and praise.

I wish I could spend more time visiting schools since the children I see are going to be the future dog owners. If only we could educate them about animals and their care we could eventually see a big decline in the overcrowded dogs' homes. Owners come to me with problems because they acquired the wrong dog, or they had no idea how to educate the puppy. Give children a basic understanding of the responsibilities involved in dog ownership, a little under-standing of how dogs should be treated and fewer dogs would be homeless. I sometimes come across children who are afraid of dogs, and they may turn out as dog-hating adults. A little care and time will usually help these children over their fear. Most who are afraid of dogs have learned the fear from their parents. I would love to see an animal education teacher who could travel around schools inform-ing and teaching the pupils.

I still miss taking Bracken on talks with me; in fact I still miss Emma. All the dogs after Emma seem to be substitutes. I never taught Emma tricks to show the audience but then she could show any dog a thing or two. In her job she did not need tricks. However many clever things I teach Psyche to do she will never match up to Emma. There will never be another Emma, not for me. Maybe that is one of the reasons why I am so motivated to train dogs, because I know what they are capable of given the correct training. Emma's capacity for learning was insatiable, her understanding of words, the names of shops, bus stations and various routes – she never stopped learning. I now realise how very little I knew of the canine brain when I had Emma and took her brilliance for granted. I look back and wonder how she was able to learn and remember with such reliability.

Dogs have difficulty picking up words. They are more adept at remembering situations. Dinner is served in the kitchen at five o'clock, for example, walks happen when the lead is taken off the peg, biscuits are given at bedtime for which the dog will sit and give a paw. We build the dog's knowledge of what happens in a regular daily situation and the dog learns that very quickly. Our dogs have realised the theme tune from *Prisoner Cell Block H* means it is bedtime, and they rush to the back door. It only took a couple of weeks for this to register because each time the programme ended I would stand up and say, "Everybody out." If the theme music is played at any other time it causes confusion. The other afternoon it was played on the radio at about three thirty and the dogs looked up from their slumbers. Katy half slithered off the chair, Pip gave a little bark of excitement and then they decided it was a hoax and went back to sleep.

There are many things Emma did that I can't equate with canine behaviour and intelligence. One instance sticks in my mind which I find hard to fathom. I listened to a lot of "talking" books when I could not see; these are books read on to tape especially for blind people. They came through the post in containers that did not require a stamp since mail for the blind is always handled free by the post office. I made regular trips with Emma to our local post office to send the books back. I could have put them into the letter box, but the lady at the post office was an Emma fan and she asked me to come in so she could say hello to Emma. One day when we went to return a book the usual lady had gone on holiday, so I passed the book over the counter. The temporary staff were obviously not used to dealing with post for the blind and refused to accept the parcel unless I put a stamp on, so I decided it was easier to pop the book in the letter box rather than try to explain the system.

A few days later I had another book to post, so I told Emma to find the post office for me. It had slipped my mind that the temporary staff would be there for the week but not Emma's. She took me straight to the letter box outside. I could explain her actions by saying we had done that the last time we posted a book and Emma had remembered, but three days later, when my next book was ready for posting, she did not take me to the letter box but into the post office. Our usual lady was back from her holiday. Was that a coincidence, or did Emma know she would be there? It was only one of many instances I can recall which does not fit in with the canine intelligence and behaviour patterns.

I wish I could find a dog with half Emma's intelligence but I will have to put up with ordinary dogs. Dealing with "ordinary" dogs spurs me on to teach them as much as possible, for fun and the challenge. I felt pleased with myself that I had taught Psyche to "speak" and now I wanted to teach her something else. Bracken had learnt to yawn and open and close his mouth as if he were talking, so I set out to teach Psyche the same. I soon hit a snag. It had been so simple to teach this to Bracken because he is always yawning. I watched him constantly and every time he yawned I gave the command and then a titbit, but Psyche did not yawn. Back to the drawing board. If she did not yawn then I had to find a different approach. I would teach her to open her mouth on command. Food is Psyche's motivation and to get the food she had to open her mouth – which is how I began. A titbit of food near her nose and each time she opened her mouth in an effort to get the titbit I gave her the command and then the titbit. It took four weeks before she actually knew what I wanted her to do, but I achieved my goal and I am wondering what I can teach her next.

I am at home most of the time so I am close to the dogs, but Emma and I were together twenty-four hours a day, seven days a week, and I am sure that had a lot to do with her learning capacity. We went everywhere together and getting to the right destination was a reward in itself for Emma. Dogs are not allowed in shops these days, so I don't take any of them shopping with me. They go out for their walk, Pip goes to dog shows and Psyche comes with me on talks, but that is only a part of my life. Emma knew everyone I knew, she was familiar with all the places I visited, every shop must have been fixed in her mind as it was in mine. I firmly believe that true understanding came between Emma and I because we were literally never apart.

CHAPTER 17

When I began to take an interest in animal welfare, at about the age of fourteen, I was anti the RSPCA. All I ever heard about this charity, from the media, was about how many dogs it had destroyed. These reports made a deep and lasting impression on me and I concluded that the RSPCA was nothing but a glorified dog murderer. I would never give money to the charity, firmly believing it did more harm than good.

Often views developed when young continue well into adult life and for many years I buried my head in the sand every time the RSPCA was mentioned. I had decided that it killed too many animals.

Writing my weekly pets column brought me in direct contact with the RSPCA, and the light dawned. The RSPCA is not the culprit. The horrible truth is that the destruction of dogs and cats is caused by irresponsible, ignorant people. Genuine reasons for a dog or cat needing a new home account for very few of the unwanted pets.

Since I realised this I have given my support to the RSPCA, but until recently I had never visited the local shelter for I knew the effect it would have on me. I felt guilty about my attitude. I was closing my eyes to the reality I did not want to know.

Eventually I plucked up courage and arranged a visit to enable me to write about the organisation's work in the *Post*. I was absolutely dreading that Monday afternoon. I was a reporter, I told myself as Rosemary and I travelled to the shelter. Reporters need to write about all types of horrific events and I must view the whole episode from an outsider's point of view, I must not get emotionally involved.

As we drew up outside the shelter Rosemary looked at me very seriously before getting out of the car.

"This is not going to be a pleasant experience. I've been here before, you know."

"I'm all right. I have a job to do and will look at everything as any other reporter would."

The staff were pleased to see me, especially as I had put off my visit for so long, and we followed one of them down to the kennel blocks. In my head I was repeating my promise to myself about not getting emotionally involved and I felt quite brave and in control as we rounded the corner. As I stepped up to look into the first run a big, black German Shepherd cross leapt at the wire begging for love and attention. That did it. I just stood and sobbed.

I felt very stupid, but I could not help it. It broke my heart to see so many dogs needing someone to love them. I was astonished at the number of pedigree dogs – Rottweilers, Dobermans, German Shepherds. Seeing the cruelty cases was almost unbearable, dogs so thin that every bone was showing; dogs covered in sores; litters of puppies which had been dumped. No matter how cruelly the dogs had been treated, they still welcomed me with trust and hope. Then there were the cats, including one who had been rescued from a river tied up in a sack. I cannot comprehend that my own species could be capable of such neglect and cruelty. It makes me ashamed to be human. Apart from the unwanted dogs and cats there were rabbits, gerbils, geese, and a flock of swans suffering from lead poisoning.

I despaired. Will we ever become civilised?

The accommodation for the animals was excellent, roomy kennels with runs for the dogs, a pond for the swans. The staff who work at the shelter have my admiration and they do everything possible to make the animals in their care happy. What they can't do is stop people being cruel and abandoning their pets. It must be soul-destroying to work so hard and with such dedication, yet be unable to stop the never-ending flow of discarded pets.

"What do you feel," I asked one of the girls, "when people bring in a dog that they are just fed up with?"

"We have to be pleasant, no matter how we feel. If we were abusive these owners wouldn't come and they would more than likely dump the dog. We are here to help the animals. The public think we don't care and have no emotions, but if they knew how much we personally suffer when we have to put an animal down perhaps then they would understand."

She did not need to explain further. For a moment I saw the sadness and despair.

"We do find a lot of good homes," the girl went on. "And it is marvellous to see those dogs taken and loved."

That remark told me why she worked at the shelter. There were the happy endings and the pleasure in finding homes for discarded pets. I was interested to know the reasons owners gave when leaving a pet at the shelter and the reply was the depressingly familiar catalogue: the dog started chewing up the home; he barked too much; he was uncontrollable; he had bitten someone; the family was going on holiday. All the dogs I had seen were normal, friendly, outgoing animals who needed a responsible owner.

I hope that at some future time I will visit the shelter again, one day when I have room for another dog.

I am relieved I am no longer breeding dogs. The few litters

we had were wonderful and taught me much about the development of puppies, which has helped me to understand the canine brain, but there are too many puppies for sale and too few responsible homes. Returning to my pack of seven healthy, contented dogs relieved a little of the grief. At least none of them would end up at the shelter.

When Don came in from the surgery for his tea, he looked round the kitchen and then in the dog room.

"You didn't bring anything home then?"

"No, but I will when we have space."

Don's eyes lit up. "Do they have any German shorthaired Pointers?"

"Not at the moment, luckily."

I really could not cope with any more pets and having too many would be irresponsible. I can just cope with the ones we have if I work hard. I promised Don, though, that in the sad event of losing Teak we would not buy a pup but find an unwanted adult.

I often look at Pip and worry about what might have happened to him if he had not had the good fortune to be born in our home. He may not have the perfect temperament but to me he is everything I could want and the pleasure he gives me out walking and going to dog shows is all I could ask for.

I view the weekend shows as time off when I can sit and relax away from the hurly-burly of telephones and vacuum cleaners. At a show I can talk dogs with fellow competitors to my heart's content. I take these days out very seriously as far as comfort is concerned and I invested in a small tent and foldable chairs. The tent is shelter from wind and rain, but more to the point it is a gathering place for everyone pops in for a chat. I pride myself in my speed and ability at putting up the tent in almost any weather conditions. I can do it single-handed in about five minutes – most of the time. One show I went to, in March, proved a little difficult as there was a gale-force wind blowing as I tried to assemble my temporary home. I had managed to erect the frame without too much of a problem, but every time I pegged one side of the cover into the ground the other side blew into the air, taking the frame with it. One mighty gust took the whole lot, with me inside hanging on to poles and canvas. The wind dropped, the tent dropped and I was buried in the middle, metal legs everywhere. I dared not let go as I knew I would lose the tent, so I had to stay there until some kind competitors saw the predicament I was in and extricated me. Pip had been watching this from the car window a few feet away, and as I emerged he gave a little squeak of delight and grinned as if to say, Great entertainment. What do you do for an encore?

I have learnt to manage quite well at dog shows, despite my poor vision. Most fellow competitors know about it and are good natured about any mistakes I make, even to claiming their dog as I did that windy day in March. The wind has a tendency to fog up my contact lens. A few blinks and it corrects itself but it always seems to happen at a critical moment. Part of the competition includes out-of-sight stays which the dogs competing in the class do together, so there are about fifty to sixty in the ring. We had left our dogs in the down stay and hidden behind a hedge. When we were called back the wind was full in my face and I could hardly see where I was going. I saw a black blob and headed for it, but as I stepped up to it someone whispered in my ear, "That's my dog you're standing next to. Your dog is over there."

Pip loves going to shows. Dogs have a wonderful memory for places, people and other dogs. Emma would remember routes we had not used for years, and she never forgot a person she had met. When I first had her I contacted her puppy walker, Paddy Wansborough, and we corresponded for two years before I actually met her. When Emma saw Paddy after all that time she went mad with delight and for a good fifteen minutes she danced around her. Pip seems to have this type of memory. I am sure most dogs do, despite the fact that many animal behaviourists say once an animal has left its parents, brothers and sisters it will not recognise them again. Pip recognises his sister, Minka. We only meet Minka and her owner, Joy, at the shows and after Minka left us at six weeks old Pip did not see her again for about a year. He is not very keen on other dogs so it is obvious when he likes one. At shows he greets his sister with squeaks of delight. This friendliness extends to his cousins, uncles and aunts, and he definitely knows they belong to our pack. Logan, Pip's uncle, often visits. Normally Pip would not allow another male into the house but he welcomes Logan like a child would welcome a favourite uncle, and fawns all over him. His friends do not include Pip's father, however, who lives a few doors down the road. If Pip sees him in the park his hackles rise, his tail stands up over his back and he takes the stiff-leg-attack pose until Ben has passed by.

I have to smile as I see Ben's receding tail. "If it had not been for him," I tell Pip, "you would be nonexistent." And what a lot of pleasure I would have been denied.

CHAPTER 18

It is quite rare for a talk to be booked for a Saturday evening, but one November this happened. Being a Saturday, Don was able to take me and we were both looking forward to our night out together in Birmingham. The function was a dinner with special guests including the Lord Mayor and Members of Parliament. I can guarantee bad weather when travelling with Don and November is notorious for fog, but as we set off from Nottingham all was well.

Not a hint of fog as we travelled down the M42 with the moon shining silvery and clear. Then we took the M6 and the fog fell from nowhere and surrounded us in a thick yellow blanket.

"Damn it," Don muttered over the steering wheel as he peered into the fog, "I'm sure that was our turnoff. I didn't see the sign until it was too late."

We motored on in silence at about ten miles an hour.

"I think we had better get off as soon as we can. This is hopeless. I can't see a thing."

At that moment I switched the radio on.

"Keep off the M6," the DJ said. "If you are already on that motorway you are advised to take the first exit off. Traffic is building up, motorists have abandoned their cars on the hard shoulder."

Don managed to locate the next turnoff, but the fog was just as thick and we had no idea where we were. For a while we wandered aimlessly in circles, Don trying to find a sign, but nothing could penetrate the fog. I was due at the talk at seven thirty and it was then seven forty-five. I never panic; it doesn't do any good and they certainly could not start the talk without me, although they might start the meal.

Don was getting more and more frustrated as we circled the outskirts of Birmingham. "There's a taxi firm. I'll pull in and ask if they will guide us."

To Don's further frustration the taxi firm had withdrawn its cabs and no amount of persuasion would get them out.

Eight fifteen, I noted. Don sat behind the wheel and gave a big sigh. "I don't think we're going to make it. I don't know Birmingham in ordinary weather, let alone this lot."

"Let's have one more crack at it. After all, whichever way we go we will be in the fog."

"Okay, I'll try that way. I don't think we've been down there." He nosed the car slowly left at an island and hugged the kerb. "We could be in luck," Don suddenly announced. "We've just passed a police station. If I can find somewhere to park the car we can go and ask for directions."

We found a safe little back street to tuck the car in and went back to the police station.

They were absolutely wonderful. "I doubt you'll find your way in this pea soup," the constable commented. "Lots of people are lost and there are cars abandoned everywhere." He picked up his helmet. "I'll lead you. It's not far."

We followed the police car for about fifteen minutes and arrived at our destination.

"How about that, petal?" Don grinned at me. "A police escort! I bet you've never arrived at a talk with a police escort before."

We both thanked the policeman profusely. Our British police force must be the best in the world.

We were over an hour late, but then so were most people. The fog seemed to be covering the whole of Birmingham.

Don and I took our place at the top table, delighted we had actually made it, until Don thought about the journey home.

"Forget about it," I told him. "Enjoy your meal. We may be lucky and it could have cleared."

The lady sitting on my right began to chat to me during the meal. She put me off my food somewhat when she asked me what I was doing there.

"I'm the speaker," I said.

"Oh, I see." And then with great authority she added, "You won't be speaking for long, will you?"

"I normally talk for about an hour."

"Goodness me, that's far too long! Maybe ten minutes."

I was aghast. Ten minutes! After the problems we had getting there I was only worth ten minutes!

During the meal the secretary came to introduce herself.

"I've been told you only want me to speak for ten minutes," I said to her.

"Ten minutes? I hope not! I expected you to speak for about an hour."

I explained that the lady next to me had told me to keep my speech short. She gave her a sidelong glance and then whispered to me, "She has nothing to do with it. She's just a guest."

A guest, I thought, who did not want to hear me.

When I rose to my feet I felt rather daunted by the idea that someone in the audience wanted to get away early. I soon pushed the thought to the back of my mind as I got the audience laughing. I told them of our problems locating the venue. Emma never had any problems, even in the fog. Her nose would take us anywhere. I recalled one evening leaving work in thick fog. Everyone was panicking in the office, the city buses had stopped running and no one could see where they were going. Emma and I had a fifteen-minute walk from our place of work to home and three of the office staff who lived in our direction followed us. They were totally hopeless in the fog. Unlike Emma and I they had no idea of how many roads they crossed each day, or the pavement textures of different areas. They could look instead. Only one weather condition put Emma off, and that was rain. In the mornings I knew if it was raining before going outside because Emma stayed in bed until the last minute. I would open the back door and she would stand on the doorstep until I physically pushed her out. Admittedly, once her harness was on she would venture into the wet, but under protest. I wasn't keen on the rain myself because I seemed to hit the puddles and get soaking wet. It wasn't until a sighted friend came home with me for tea one evening, when it was raining, that I discovered why. Emma was so intent on keeping her paws out of the puddles she walked me through them.

The fog had not cleared later that evening and it took us four hours to cover the sixty miles home, Don getting more and more uptight about the conditions. I tried to placate him by saying that however much he moaned about the fog it would not go away, but in the end I gave up and went to sleep.

I am fortunate to have Rosemary to drive me to most of my talks. As they are usually at lunchtime Don is at work, which is a blessing considering what he is like on long journeys. Rosemary is the opposite, calm and collected. We make the drive leisurely, often stopping for a cuppa or to savour the view. On the odd occasion Rosemary is unable to take me I ask Peter, an old friend. He has a tailor's shop in Stapleford. The nice thing about living in a small community is that everyone knows everyone and shopping is more a tour of friends than a buying trip. Don would not have much call to visit the tailor's but he met Peter and his partner, John, when buying a shirt and they have become firm friends. Peter is a calm driver. I have never seen him get ruffled over anything and he is as placid as a Labrador. I have seen him get embarrassed, though, for people mistake him for my husband and ask him all kinds of personal questions. I try to remember now to introduce him before I start my talk. On one occasion we had quite a lot of fun when I tried to describe the relationship. Peter was sitting on my left at the top table.

"I must explain before I start my talk," I began, waving a hand towards Peter, "this is Peter and I am not married to him." The audience started to laugh. "No, it's not like that," I protested. "I'm already married, but not to Peter." The audience had hysterics. I could see I was getting in deeper and deeper. "No, no," I tried again, "Peter and I are just good friends." That finished them off and I could not stop them laughing for about five minutes. I think I managed to explain the relationship to them, eventually.

Laughter is wonderful and if I can start the audience laughing I know I have them for the rest of the talk. It's fine if I can get them laughing but it is another matter if it is me who wants to laugh. Smiling at the audience works wonders, but not giggling. One talk I gave was done completely with suppressed giggles from me. The lady who introduced me somehow got mixed up on her names and told the audience, with conviction, that I was Ethel Scott. I politely corrected her, because I did not fancy being referred to as Ethel, but I desperately wanted to laugh. All the way through my talk I kept thinking about this Ethel: who was she, and did I really look like an Ethel? After the talk I rushed out to the car and as Rosemary started up the engine I began to laugh uncontrollably.

It is amazing how dogs respond to laughter like humans do. After I have delivered my talk it is Psyche's turn. She barks her age and plays dead dog but one of her favourite tricks is the hankie one. If I sneeze she finds the hankie and gives it to me. I normally set this up by putting the hankie hanging out of my sleeve or pocket and once, as soon as I had finished my talk, Psyche produced it. When I realised she had anticipated the cue I sneezed anyway, and that made the trick even better for the audience took it that Psyche knew I was going to sneeze even before I did.

The art of being a public speaker is to be able to turn events to advantage. I have learnt how to do this over the years and even the most embarrassing things can get a laugh if handled correctly. I had raved about sight to an audience, saying most sighted people do not use their eyes and look about them. "I try not to miss a minute of sight so I can take in every bit of visual information I can lay my eyes on." I had told them. "I try to remember that each day should be viewed as the most exciting visual experience in life, as if it is the only day I will ever get to see the world." I tried to make them understand my sight is not perfect. I don't see detail or distance but I use the sight I have to great advantage and I said I hoped from then on they would look at everything carefully. Next to me on the table was a tray with a jug of water and a glass on it. After an hour of nonstop talking I am always dying of thirst so I reached down, picked up the jug and poured water into the glass – or so I thought. The water shot out, soaking my dress and giving Psyche a good drench. The glass was upside down. Having just lectured the audience about not using their eyes I felt very stupid and for a moment lost for words. The audience sat silently waiting for me to say something. Handled incorrectly the situation could have ruined my whole talk. I can't see plain glass and at home I have broken more drinking glasses than I can remember. I did not want to tell my audience that – the last thing I want is people feeling sorry for me – but I knew I had to get a laugh. I took the glass and turned it over.

"At home our glasses have little labels on the bottom reading, 'Other way up'."

I never tire of telling people how wonderful it is to see, and about Emma. It is fifteen years since she retired as a guide-dog and yet when I am in front of an audience I can recall each minute of our time together. I don't just stand there and talk, I relive everything again and again. I love telling people of Emma's ability as a guide-dog and her uncanny knack of finding places. One of the funniest things I enjoy relating, is the Boots episode.

When I worked in Nottingham Emma and I used to shop at lunchtime, but Emma had a free run first in the local park. I put her harness on one day after her run and told her we were going to Boots the chemist. This entailed a five-minute walk through the centre of Nottingham. Emma knew exactly where Boots was, so I left it to her. Boots had recently turned into a self-service supermarket. I could not serve myself, but the staff knew us and Emma would take me into the shop and along to a cash-out where one of the girls would help me. On this particular occasion we had entered the shop and Emma was striding briskly up the centre when suddenly she stopped and I heard a thud. Thinking she had knocked something off a shelf I put my shopping bag down and had a feel round on the floor. There I found a huge, soggy mud-encrusted bone. Emma had obviously found this nasty object in the park and must have carried it proudly through the city. There was no way I was letting her have it. I picked up my bag and, with a warning "Leave it", I told her to find the door and we scuttled out before anyone could see what we had left in the shop.

When I couldn't see I needed to remember how many steps there were to a door, where to locate the door handle of the different shops we used and so on. My mind in those days was filled with odd information, and so was Emma's. A few weeks later I returned to Boots. The door was locked though I knew we were in the right place – two steps to the door, a long metal handle – and I pushed at the door a few times to no avail. Emma turned round and down the steps, found the crossing we always used and turned right on the other side of the road, our route back to work. I had given up my idea of shopping in Boots, but Emma hadn't. She paused, then took me into a shop which I could smell was a chemist.

"Hello, my duck," someone said. I recognised the voice, for the girl had often served me in Boots. "I saw you trying the door of our shop across the road," she went on. "We moved over here temporarily while they alter it. I was going to come and tell you but then I saw your dog reading the notice in the window."

It is wonderful to relate how clever Emma was and tell of that special bond we had. It is sad when I am asked if I still have Emma and I receive letters from all over the world from people who have just read *Emma and I.* It never ceases to amaze me that people are still interested. They want to know how Emma is, and I have the task of telling them she died in 1981. But like all loved ones we lose, her memory stays as long as I keep it alive.

CHAPTER 19

———

"He has done a thousand pounds worth of damage. If I had known how destructive he was going to be I would never have had him. In fact, my husband is threatening to get rid of him," Mrs Miller confessed.

The five-month-old yellow Labrador gazed up at me with sad brown eyes. His owner had come to me in despair for the pup had done nothing but chew from the day he was taken to his new home with the Millers.

"We got a Labrador because we thought they were well behaved. They train them as guide-dogs, don't they? And those beautiful pups on the toilet roll ad look so cute."

James seemed cute enough at the moment sitting in my lounge, but I know all too well the havoc and destruction a Labrador puppy can cause. This little fellow was under threat of losing his home if he did not stop trying to destroy it. While I had some sympathy for his owner my true sympathy lay with James. He had no idea what he had done wrong. Why shouldn't he chew up the settee and eat the carpet? No one complained when he shredded the toys and bones he was given.

Before I allowed prospective owners to take one of my puppies I made sure they realised Labradors are not saints. Yes, they do make good guide-dogs, after intensive training, and those pups seen on TV are probably little devils when the camera is turned off.

Why do people buy puppies because they see them on television? The same fate has befallen the Old English sheep dog. This breed can look beautiful when groomed and well cared for, but what potential owners do not realise is how much work is involved in keeping a long coat clean. An Old English only needs to take a walk in the rain and he is covered in mud, and his coat gets matted and smelly without constant grooming.

"He doesn't like being brushed," is an excuse I often hear from owners whose poor dogs are matted and dirty, but no dog would like being groomed when its fur is full of knots.

I don't blame the advertisers for using dogs. One might as well blame guide-dog trainers for using Labradors, because the popularity of the Labrador has come about mainly because of their work as guide-dogs. I blame breeders and the stupid people who buy a pup just because they have seen it on TV. Dog ownership should be thought about as carefully as having a baby. Dogs take nearly as much patience to rear, though their plus is that they grow up more quickly than children. Education must be the answer to stop people buying the wrong kind of dog for their needs as the wrong match can cause great heartache. I see old ladies who want a dog to cuddle and love and to ease the loneliness, but sometimes the love and devotion the lonely pour on to their pets has drastic results. The dog turns out to be dominant and in no time at all is threatening the owner. I hate having to tell these owners that if they want to keep the dog and not get bitten they must not allow it to sleep on the bed, and nor can they cuddle it as much as they would like to.

I remember one lady who visited me with a Shih Tzu dog. Her husband had bought him for her as a wedding anniversary present and three months later the husband had died. All her love had been channelled in to the dog, the one connection she had with her late husband. Sadly the dog had become aggressive towards her. It is soul-destroying for owners to find their companion turning against them and the grief this causes lonely people is almost as bad as losing a loved one. At times like these I need to be careful, patient and calm. I try very hard to tell the owner that their dog needs to have a pack leader, someone he can trust and look up to. I explain that most dogs do not really want to lead the pack and it will actually be a big relief to him when he accepts a subordinate place. I do not know what I would do if I could not have a dog sleep in our bedroom and I am not a lonely person, but luckily for me I have dogs who will not take advantage of the privilege.

Emma and I had an equal partnership. Now I know more about the temperament of dogs I can state that Emma was no pushover; she was in a way quite a dominant dog. She objected strongly to being made a fuss of and if strangers put their arms round her she would leap away in disgust (Pip does exactly the same). I respected Emma's need for independence. She would much rather I threw a toy for her than give her a cuddle. She was given every privilege a dog could have; she slept on the bed and no one would move her off a chair so they could sit down. She knew she had total control of other humans, and she used this control. When we travelled to work on the bus each day, Emma would choose her seat. She would take me down the bus until she found a place she fancied and if the seat was occupied she would stand and stare at the occupant until he or she moved. She did not have any aggression, and yet given this power over humans theoretically she should have taken advantage. A dog treated in this way would soon stop obeying the owner, it would please itself. Why didn't Emma do this? Why did she unfailingly take me everywhere I asked? Admittedly, we had some compromises and I agreed to let her do things that were breaking the rules. Sitting at kerbs was one rule guide-dog owners must stick by. The dog should wait at each kerb for the owner to give the next command. I remember Brian (my trainer at guide-dogs) saying that if we let the dogs get away with little things like not sitting at kerbs their work would deteriorate. A partnership meant keeping to the basic rules. Emma didn't keep to the rules, not when it was raining she didn't; no way would she sit at kerbs when the ground was wet and when it was raining she took a detour into every shop entrance to be dry for a few seconds. Oh, yes. I remember another rule of Emma's: we did not pass a butcher's shop. She knew every butcher's shop within a ten-mile radius of home and she had been in each.

I was poignantly reminded of Emma's rule about butchers when I found an old video tape tucked in the bookcase which had some footage of Emma on it taking me through Nottingham in the early seventies. Someone had filmed us and I had had it transferred on to a video. Fearing I might record over this most treasured tape by accident, I had hidden it behind some books. I smiled when I saw Emma pause outside the big butcher's shop in the square. Normally she would not have taken no for an answer and dragged me in, but she knew she was being filmed. She gave the shop a longing look, licked her muzzle and continued. On the same tape I found some footage of the dogs taking part in a television programme in 1982. Bracken stood next to me as I talked about dog training, his tail waving, his lovely brown eyes alert and watchful, his coat gleaming like polished chestnuts. He was so handsome and youthful and now the poor old lad has aged dreadfully. He has a bad back leg, one eye has a cataract and his coat has lost that beautiful bloom and faded to a dusty brown flecked with grey. Teak, Buttons, Mocha and Katy sat round me while I did the interview. A young Teak gazed at me from the screen, her nose constantly testing the air currents, every muscle in her body ready for the chase. Katy was full of inquisitiveness, her bright eyes watching every move the interviewer made, her two front paws constantly dancing, keen to be off and running. Mocha and Buttons' coats shone with ginger tints, although I confess that Mocha sat staring somewhere off camera, oblivious to her surroundings.

It was wonderful to see them young and fit, and yet at the same time it broke my heart not to be able to stretch out a hand and touch Emma. How cruel it is that dogs don't live as long as we do. Especially Emma, because she was not like a dog. She was different from any dog I have ever met. She had a sense of humour, a human's understanding of words and fair play. She took care of me and in return I took care of her. No, there will never be another Emma. Dogs don't come like that.

It has taken me a long time to adapt to real dogs and face the truth about the pack instinct and the fact that every dog is not perfect – and nor, of course, is every owner. If only people would think more carefully before buying a dog. Many buy the wrong dog, and many others should never be allowed to have one at all. At least the people who bring their dogs to me care; they are trying to correct their animals' behaviour, unlike the hundreds that give up and get rid of them.

In an ideal world all dogs should be registered so some type of control would be possible. I would like to see a hefty licence or registration fee of around fifty pounds for a puppy which would drop to a nominal sum of say five pounds annually when the dog had been castrated or the bitch spayed. Working dogs and senior citizens' dogs would be exempt. This would cut down unwanted pups and stop impulse buying, assuming that the licence would be purchased at the same time as the puppy. The problem is that we do not live in an ideal world and such a scheme could not be implemented. We, the true dog lovers, would pay through the nose to cover those irresponsible people who avoided paying, and they would be the ones with uncontrollable dogs. I do not see why I should underwrite the bad owners, although, of course, the honest who buy their television licence and pay their road tax will always be subsidising those who don't pay.

There are various suggestions in the press at the moment about how dogs should be kept under control. Muzzles have been proposed, and that dogs should be kept on leads. To me these restrictions would totally ruin the pleasure I have taking my dogs out. I think it would be cruel, not only to the dogs but to responsible owners. I have a better way of making irresponsible owners pay: ban them from having dogs. Sometimes this happens for a limited period, but I was astonished to read that an owner with a Rottweiler which had attacked a child was paying a fine of twenty-one pounds a week for having a dangerous dog. If our laws permit people to keep a dog which has damaged a child then there is something drastically wrong. No matter how much the owner is prepared to pay in fines he has proved to be irresponsible and should not be allowed to have a dog at all.

CHAPTER 20

―――――――――

"Look at Mocha." Don attracted my attention away from my Open University study book. Mocha was sitting at the end of the settee, gazing fixedly at a spot on the carpet. I was just about to go back to my book – after all Mocha was doing what she always did – but Don said, "No, keep looking."

I did. Mocha's front paws began to slide slowly forwards, her eyes closing. Then suddenly she shook herself, sat up straight and resumed her stare at the carpet. A minute or two elapsed and off she went again paws slipping, eyelids drooping.

"I wonder what she is thinking about? Whatever it is she is putting a lot of mental effort into it. Maybe," Don added, smiling, "she is a lot more intelligent than we think. She could be working out Einstein's theory of relativity."

"Perhaps, but obviously she's stuck. Maybe she's got to the bit about travelling faster than the speed of light. If we could do that we would meet ourselves coming back."

"How's that?" Don asked me seriously.

"I haven't a clue. It's only theory."

At that moment Mocha hit the floor, nose first. A normal dog would have been shocked at this, but Mocha just rolled over and lay, paws waving, as if that had been her original intention. After a quick carpet shuffle, rubbing her back across the floor, she came to tell me she wanted to go out. I got up, opened the back door for her and decided to wait rather than return to my book. She pottered out into the yard and then sat with her back to me.

"Hurry up, Mocha." Without looking round she swished her tail along the slabs, but did not offer to get on with anything. "Mocha, either come in or do something. I'm not standing here all night." She swished her tail again, clambered to her feet, walked into the house and resumed her position on the settee. "I don't know about that dog," I told Don. "I am sure she is going senile."

"Do dogs go senile?"

"They must. People do, so odds on dogs do. Mocha certainly has."

I sat and viewed our seven dogs: Mocha an old, senile Labrador, Bracken blind in one eye and only one good back leg, Katy with her cataracts, Buttons suffering from emphysema. Teak, well Teak isn't doing too badly for her age though she has the odd limp here and there. Five out of the seven are old codgers. I seem to do nothing but hand out pills and visit the vet. Oh, I would not be without any of them, but age is catching up with them. I should have left about a four-year gap between dogs and ideally four would be plenty to look after. I certainly intend to have other dogs, but it will be some time before a new puppy comes into our home.

I have learned and benefited much from owning dogs. They have proved to me that love and kindness pay off, not only with pets but with people also. I used to be one of the old school of thinkers regarding attitudes to violence, aggression and dominance. If you asked me what I thought of criminals or naughty children my answer would have been to give them a good hiding or make them work hard. It is only because I have studied canine behaviour that I now realise how humans will respond to violence and aggression. I have learnt from my understanding of pack law that people have the same tendencies as dogs. The emotions and motives may be well hidden but they are within all of us to some degree.

I find myself looking at people and categorising their temperaments as I do the dogs. I am often astonished to discover that someone I have always regarded as meek and mild is really a very cleverly dominant person. A simple example is the seating arrangements in my own lounge. Don's chair is the tallest with a winged back and is strategically placed in the corner near the fire and facing the television. His chair and its position show who is the more dominant partner, and more than that: when Don is not in the lounge I tend to use the chair, especially when I am talking to the dog owners who visit me. Sitting in that chair I feel in charge of the situation. I tested this theory out by sitting somewhere else when I had a consultation and it made me feel most uncomfortable. This positioning, you may think, is only noticed by me but that is not the case. When we have friends visit who are dominant they head for Don's chair, if they get the opportunity, whereas the submissive visitor will choose somewhere else to sit.

I have begun to see how we females make our men and children dominant. We put their dinner on the table first (the pack leader always gets his food first). The man goes out to hunt (earn the money), the female stays home tending the pack area and young. Some men do not like their wives going out to work, and the saying, "A woman's place is in the home", is a man's way of asserting his authority as a dog would do in a wild pack.

I am not a dominant person; in fact I find it difficult to establish any kind of dominance over people. If someone pushes in front of me in a shop to get served first I will back off. Good manners? No, submission.

I have learned a tremendous amount about my own character through my work and have been able to help myself overcome various traits. I suppose if I were a dog I would be nervous aggressive: afraid of strangers, showing aggression to keep them at bay. In human terms this temperament has come out a little differently. I do not threaten to bite a stranger although I am rather intimidated by people I do not know. To disguise my nerves I use overconfidence and talk and laugh a lot. In difficult situations I can quake inside but exude great confidence. Take dog shows as an example: being in the ring is a gruelling few minutes because I am being scrutinised by a judge who is looking for faults. I found that although I enjoyed training the dogs and the convivial day out I dreaded going in to the ring to work my dog. I literally shook with nerves because at the end of the round the judge would criticise. Even if this was done nicely, with a smile, it was still criticism. Not being a very confident person it left me feeling hopeless, useless. Now I understand how to deal with this so I can enjoy competing. The judge is there to criticise, to find the dog with the least faults. My attitude is to pick up any good points about Pip's work and forget the bad, to be proud and confident and smile. The benefits are enormous. If I make mistakes in the ring, such as walking into the ropes, or at talks pouring water on to upturned glasses, the best thing to do for morale is to laugh about it. Forget one's shortcomings and push the good points to the fore. Dogs do not criticise themselves or have feelings of remorse or guilt. Guilt is probably one of man's (and woman's) worst handicaps in life.

Dogs are honest creatures. They do not try to deceive or cover up character defects. The human being is the only living creature on the planet capable of deceit. Sometimes I think we need our dogs far more than they need us. I certainly need them for support, especially if I am giving a talk. I can stand in front of an audience or a television camera and look confident and I need a dog like some women need make-up. Often this can be quite a hassle and the speaker-finders are astonished when I tell them that not only will I be accompanied by a driver but I will also have a dog with me.

"I didn't think you needed a guide-dog any more," they say.

"No, I don't, but I have to bring a dog with me."

"What will it do while we eat? There's nowhere near the hotel to let a dog run and the room we meet in is upstairs."

Many organisers try to put me off but I stand firm and so far we have both been accepted.

I still feel naked if I go out dogless. I can't take one to my evening classes for the Open University and I'd like to believe this is why I failed the science course, but it was more than that. The maths was bad enough but when we came to reading maps and doing experiments I was sunk. I tried hard to understand the mathematical and scientific jargon and attended the classes each week in the hope I would learn, but that was my first downfall. I had to travel to Nottingham on my own, dogless, in the dark (horror of horrors), but I was prepared to face the ordeal in an effort to learn. What I was not prepared to face was the classroom situation. There were about twelve students, all of whom seemed to know each other. We sat behind desks and the tutor stood at the front of the classroom, and behind her, stretching along the wall, was a blackboard. I could feel myself panicking at the very sight of the board. I was a child again at the mercy of the other kids and the teachers. Most of the teachers were kind and helped whenever they could, but some of them had as much feeling as a rhino. I still shudder at the memory of one teacher in the junior school who slapped me round the head for knocking a jar of water over. It was pointless my telling him I did not see it, and anyway in those days one did not speak to teachers unless asked.

When the Open University tutor began to draw on the blackboard, showing how to work out the speed at which earthquake waves travel through the earth's layers, I froze in terror. I wanted to bury my face in my hands and sob. I thought this type of experience was behind me. I may be able to see much more than I could as a child, but I could not see the blackboard and nothing would have got me to admit it. As for going out and looking closely – well, wild horses would not have dragged me. I find it hard to admit to people that my sight is limited. I don't mind having a laugh about it when I am giving a talk, but where it means I am not as capable as others I keep quiet. I am sure my attitude goes back to my schooldays when I longed to be the same as everyone else. Consequently I would often lie when asked if I could see this or that and I still do it. When the tutor asked me if everything was clear regarding the mathematics of quake waves I nodded my head and bit my lip. I bowed out gracefully after racking my brains for weeks on how to establish the speed of earthquake waves travelling through the earth's layers.

I felt inadequate about my failure, but that is no way forward. Defeat is not a word I recognise and so I changed to a social sciences course. At the moment I am studying the cause and possible cures of vandalism. Back to the pack instinct again. Maybe if one could use some of the controls for dogs on people we may achieve the perfect world, but taking a vandal's possessions away or preventing him from going upstairs could have drastic consequences. I think I need to know a little more about the complexity of the human mind before I see problem people.

The social science course is far easier for me. There are no graphs or maths to contend with and the Open University does everything possible to enable blind people to study. I can see to read, and I love reading, but my speed is very slow as I have to look at each letter and I have a type of word blindness. I can't retain the spelling of words in my head. I check in the dictionary for the correct spelling and by the time I close the book and pick up a pen I have forgotten how the word was spelt. My work on this course is on tapes, which helps me to keep up the studying required each week. My aim is a degree in psychology. I would prefer animal psychology, but there is no such course available so humans will have to do. I must remember, though, that when I am writing my essays for the tutor I am referring to people. My first essay on vandalism was returned with the comment, "You have referred to vandals as packs, packs are animals not people." Perhaps that is open to conjecture.

Daily I am learning more and more about the human and the canine brain. I set myself targets of training and try methods of motivation. This year I am keeping a daily record of Pip's ball motivation and his attitude to work, or should I say play? I gain so much enjoyment out of playing with him and taking him to shows and often wish I could give up everything else to have more time for dog activities.

Apart from the talks I get asked to attend functions, open garden fetes and so on. I go whenever possible, especially if the function is geared to raising money or helping the disabled. On Friday 2 March the sun shone and the fields beckoned, and I wanted to be walking the dogs instead of being at a conference on the employment of disabled persons. I had been asked to give a short talk to local employers to encourage them to hire blind people. I was convinced the whole thing would be a rather stuffy affair but agreed to attend because I thought it may help employers give a little more consideration to disabled applicants. On the morning I regretted having taken it on. Work at home was piling up, the mail covered the dining room table, the ironing lay waiting and, of course, there was always the housework. I didn't even have time to leave lunch for Don and told him he would have to go to the fish and chip shop as Psyche and I left the house. Strangely, whenever I don't want to fulfil an engagement, I end up benefiting.

The gathering turned out to be very friendly. Various

organisations were represented and there were stands showing aids to help the disabled in everyday life and give them more independence in their jobs.

The talk and Psyche went down well and great interest was shown by the employers. People came up to talk about how to help or to make a fuss of Psyche, then one young lady held out her hand.

"I am Sue. I'm one of your cousins."

I took her proffered hand in amazement. I knew I had a few cousins around the area whom I had never met. I had often felt sad we had lost touch and had thought that one day I would make an effort to find them. It was wonderful to meet Sue and we spent some time exchanging news of our families. Before I left I made sure we would not lose contact again and through Sue I would meet my other long-lost cousins. The effort of attending was worth that meeting alone but better was to come out of it.

I found the stand representing the deaf and was shown a telephone which received typed messages. I had heard about such things and it had crossed my mind that with one of them I would be able to communicate with my mother, but I had not investigated the matter further, believing the machine would cost thousands of pounds. The cost of the telephone, I was informed, was a little over a hundred and fifty pounds. It is about the size of a small typewriter and receives typewritten messages and displays them on a screen. I was thrilled to learn I could actually get two of these wonderful inventions. The revelation made the whole day worthwhile to me and I hope I never forget that doing things one may not want to do, because it is an effort, is always rewarded. Mum and I have ordered our Minicoms. There is a waiting list, but it should only be a matter of weeks now. I can't wait, after all these years, to ring mum and type out, "HELLO, MUM."